zarbo

recipes from a new zealand deli

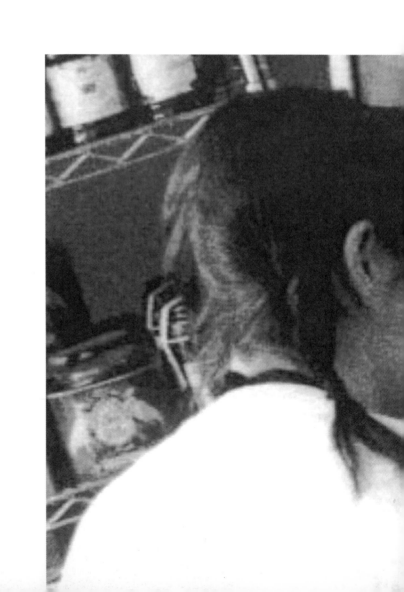

zarbo

recipes from a new zealand deli

MARK McDONOUGH and ZARBO DELI & CAFE

Photographs by Donna North

A RANDOM HOUSE BOOK
published by
Random House New Zealand
18 Poland Road, Glenfield, Auckland,
New Zealand
www.randomhouse.co.nz

Auckland
New York
Toronto
London
Sydney
Johannesburg

First published 2002, reprinted 2002, 2003

ISBN 1 86941 5345

Cover design: Thoughtfields
Photography: Donna North
Design: Thoughtfields & Random House NZ
Production: Thinking Caps, Auckland, NZ
Printed: Bookbuilders, Hong Kong

www.zarbo.co.nz

Acknowledgements
Recipe for gluten-free baking
powder on page 113
© The Allergy Bible
(Quadrille Publishing Ltd.)
reproduced by kind permission.
Instructions for preparation of
artichokes on page 18
© The Essentials of Classic
Italian Cooking, Marcella Hazan
(Knopf Publishing). Every
endeavour was made to contact
the copyright holder of this title
but without success.

contents

preface

ABOVE ALL ELSE, FOOD SHOULD BE ENJOYABLE. I first became really interested in cooking when I was a student, in the days when all flats had copies of books by Alison Holst and Digby Law on their shelves, along with the indispensable *Moosewood Cookbook*. The aim was to prepare huge filling meals for the maximum number of friends with minimum effort and cost. Parties were casual affairs with copious quantities of cheap wine, food and fun. It was then I realised that food shouldn't be taken too seriously. I hope this philosophy will encourage you to read this book with an eye to experimenting and enjoying the process of cooking and eating. Mix and match, use these recipes as a base to work from, relax and have fun!

New Zealanders are lucky to have such ready access to fresh produce and interesting flavours. The perennial Kiwi desire to travel and experience new cultures has shaped our attitudes towards the flavours we incorporate into our food. An eclectic mixture, ours is fusion cuisine with a unique antipodean twist.

Seven years ago, good speciality food stores were a rarity in Auckland. When you can't find what you want, you make it yourself, and so Zarbo was born. Influenced by the Dixon Street Deli in Wellington (one of the first delicatessens in New Zealand) and the traditional New York delis with their unique bustle and style, Zarbo aimed to be a one-stop shop for real foodies.

Innovation and tradition are equally important to Zarbo, and we invest a lot of time in travelling the world to find products and ideas to bring back to New Zealand. We import a large, unique range of fresh and packaged foods and have developed our own range of Zarbo branded products to add instant flavour to dishes. These products can now be found in more than 35 stores around the country and are making their way into Asia and Europe and Australia.

In the recipes here I've tried to give you a real taste of Zarbo, with new flavours that may seem a little foreign at first but could well become staples of your pantry. I've included some classic favourites from the Zarbo kitchen, but also food that I cook at home. After the rigours of running the deli and cafe, I find solace in my own kitchen in the evening. When I'm frazzled at the end of the day, my home cooking needs to be easy and, with a young family, it definitely needs to be quick. Most of the recipes are low in fat and in dairy products. There are also recipes for those who need to avoid wheat but don't want to sacrifice taste.

The global trend towards healthy living means people are far more questioning of what they put into their bodies than ever before. Significant understanding about food, what it contains and how it is grown, allows us to make informed choices about what we feed ourselves and our families. In this book, you'll read about my recommendations for using fresh ingredients, organics and healthy oils, and about simple ways of cooking them to retain their freshness, flavour and nutritional value. Healthy food, as well as making us feel better, just tastes better.

I could not have written this book without the sweet inspiration of Sallyann Hingston, my head baker. From the campness of her cupcakes to the decadent indulgence of her French chocolate tart, she is a star. Many thanks to Donna North for her superb photography and food styling, and to

my sister Diane Dolan for testing so many recipes to make sure they worked for the reader. (Groaning and staggering after preparing and eating so many of my sweet treats, she and her family have encouraged me to write a slimmer's cookbook next time!) Thanks also to Random House New Zealand. My gratitude to my loyal staff and customers who have helped to build the community feeling of the Zarbo stores and made the business what it is today. Finally, to Cushla and Felix, thanks for being there at the end of the day when I come home.

Mark McDonough
Zarbo Deli & Cafe
Newmarket
Auckland

introduction

ENJOYED SOME GOOD PASTA DISHES IN THE PAST COUPLE OF WEEKS? How about an Asian meal – Chinese, Japanese, perhaps Korean? Chances are you answered yes to both questions. Now transport yourself back, say, 20 years and ask these questions again and you'll realise just how much eating habits in our little triple-isled antipodean paradise have changed.

It used to be fashionable to ask whether New Zealand had a real cuisine of its own. 'Sure – meat and three veg followed by pavlova' was the cynic's response. There are still plenty of places where these Kiwi staples reign supreme, but most of us are enjoying what has become the indigenous cuisine of the new millennium – fresh local ingredients prepared in ways that borrow from both the Mediterranean and Asia.

In fact, it is hard to find a modern restaurant menu that doesn't show at least some influence from Japan, China, Indonesia or Italy for example. It might be as simple as bok choy served alongside the lamb, or a squeeze of wasabi paste in the mayonnaise, but it is often far more complex. Many of our top chefs are going all-out to create dishes that apply the philosophy of one or more Asian cuisines to the best local ingredients. The dishes they create in the process are uniquely their own, and they well deserve their exalted place in the national culinary jigsaw. Look at the recipes in this book. Kaffir lime leaves, popular in Thailand and Cambodia, are added to a Mediterranean salsa based on corn and tomatoes. Pesto, that famous Italian staple, is spiked with ginger, chilli and coriander. Lemongrass is combined with eggplant, and even risotto is 'Asianised' through the use of basmati, rather than arborio rice, and the addition of herbs like Vietnamese mint.

And why not? The food we enjoy is constantly evolving, particularly in countries as young as ours.

A good way to measure the changing Kiwi attitude to food is to look back at our entertaining and dining-out habits. In 1973 a landmark book named *Dining In and Dining Out in New Zealand*, Australian immigrant Patricia Harris talked about 'the single-handed housewife who likes to produce good and interesting food for her guests, while retaining the ability to join in the conversation, keep her powder dry and (above all else) her natural sunny disposition unruffled.'

A dinner party for six is given as 'the ideal number for a beginner', but the book points out that if seating can be found for eight, it should be possible to arrange two tables of bridge after the meal.

But not all the advice given has dated. At the end of the introduction it is written, 'Above all, never lose sight of the simple but frequently forgotten fact that it is the people who are the important ingredient of all social occasions and that, if those present are not enjoying themselves, all your trouble and planning may well be so much wasted time and money.' Some things are constant truths. The introduction to the Dining Out section is as evocative of the times as that for the Dining

In pages. 'The eating of a meal cooked by someone else and being made welcome by a head waiter whose minions will attend to the wants of the diners makes a blissful change for the busy woman who is normally in the position of performing all these duties,' it reads. The introduction then launches into a lengthy treatise on the horrors of eating in the dining room of a large hotel – described as 'the only option not so long ago'.

The menus from the various restaurants reviewed make interesting reading. Oysters mornay were popular, as was steak au poivre. Salads were likely to sport Thousand Island dressing and mushrooms could be ordered either à la Provencale or à la Grecque.

Most of our top dining establishments in the 1970s listed the bulk of their dishes in French. Cultural cringe? Partly, no doubt, but it also seems likely that the restaurateurs presumed anybody with the inclination to visit their eateries would know the classical dishes on offer by their original names. But *Dining In and Dining Out in New Zealand* was published in relatively enlightened times. A decade earlier, it was not possible to buy wine in a restaurant. To our politicians, it was seen as just another form of alcohol and therefore something to be discouraged. Stories abound of patrons sneaking in bottles that were duly opened and served in secret by the waiter, sometimes from a teapot to avoid arousing the suspicion of any lurking bureaucrats. The firm belief that alcohol of any sort was evil went back a long way. The *Official Yearbook* in 1919 listed it ahead of syphilis, epilepsy and puberty as a major cause of insanity.

Those attitudes are difficult to understand today. Wander around the restaurant areas of any New Zealand town and you will see people of all ages ordering and enjoying honest food and interesting wine with knowledge and confidence. Dining and drinking wine outdoors, once prohibited for fear of influencing the innocent young, is hugely popular right through the long days of summer and autumn. The mood is relaxing, and the food, ambience and service in the best establishments fits right in. 'By the glass' options give diners the opportunity to find the ideal wine match for each course in a multi-dish meal, and good waiters are competent enough to offer sound advice on the best combinations.

New Zealand is being recognised, at last, as an exciting destination for international foodies and the origin of much fine produce. For the last part of the 19th and most of the 20th century our food industry was almost solely in the business of sending huge amounts of protein to Britain in the form of frozen sheep carcasses, pallet-loads of butter and large blocks of cheese. In 1933, more than 50 per cent of all British imports of these three staples came from New Zealand. We started to get a bit more refined a few years later, when we at least promoted Prime Canterbury Lamb, but that still translated as frozen dead sheep.

Today's culinary exports are considerably more interesting – our wine, for example, enjoys an international reputation for excellence. And game meats, seafood, organic fruit and vegetables, free-range eggs, patés, processed products and even cakes leave our shores regularly for overseas destinations.

The country is gaining a reputation as the world's delicatessen.

antipasto

The equivalent of an appetizer, antipasto is the first course in an Italian meal. Here, it's a section in which anything goes — from dips to salsas, from traditional Italian antipasti to modern Asian-influenced dishes, I've tried to provide a multinational and versatile base to work from.

these days we're experiencing a welcome return to entertaining at home, and the kitchen is now the focal point of many households. It's in this relaxed, interactive environment that the informality of antipasti really comes to the fore. Terrifically adaptable, they make wonderful platter food and are great for entertaining. The traditional Italian antipasto platter offers a great opportunity to showcase your creative talents. Just pick up a selection of salamis, cheeses, caperberries, sun-dried tomatoes, artichokes, pickled vegetables and so on, and arrange them artfully on an attractive serving dish.

We're blessed here in New Zealand with an abundance of fresh vegetables and seafood. Juicy, flavoursome green-lipped mussels or calamari can be simply prepared by adding a few choice fresh herbs and spices. Dips and salsas served with hunks of fresh crusty bread, or crostini, make an ideal accompaniment to informal drinks.

Antipasti can also be quickly constructed to make inspired and varied entrées or lunches. Vegetable antipasti that capture your imagination can also be served as a side dish to the main meal. Antipasto dips and salsas make a good addition to main dishes. For instance, try the Romescue (p.29) on grilled fish, or the Sweetcorn Salsa (p.29) on barbecued chicken. Whichever way you look at it, by mastering a few of these basic recipes you can eat well on any occasion and at any time of day.

Cannellini Bean, Roast Garlic and Truffle Oil Dip
Makes 1-1½ cups

Pulses are an essential component of the Italian diet. This simply prepared dip is made more stunning by the addition of the truffle oil.

100 g garlic, peeled, tossed in a little olive oil and roasted in a moderate oven for approximately 30 minutes
400 g cooked cannellini beans
2 sprigs fresh rosemary, finely chopped
½ cup olive oil
juice of ½ a lemon
salt and pepper
2 teaspoons truffle oil

Put the prepared garlic, beans and rosemary into a food processor and pulse until the beans are crushed. Slowly add the olive oil and lemon juice. Season with salt and pepper. Finally add the truffle oil and blend through.

Refrigerate for a minimum of 2 hours before serving.

Asian Pesto
Makes 1 cup

The traditional Italian pesto is a staple of the Italian kitchen and should become essential to the Pacific kitchen too. The coriander and mint are enhanced by the cashew nuts and lemon juice. Try as a dip or as a sauce on noodles or on fish.

20 g fresh ginger, peeled
1 small red chilli, seeded and chopped
1 clove garlic, peeled
50 g fresh coriander
25 g fresh mint
150 g toasted, salted cashew nuts
juice of 1 lemon
½ cup peanut oil

Place the ginger, chilli and the garlic into a food processor and pulse until broken down. Add the coriander and mint and process. Add the cashew nuts and the lemon juice and process until the nuts are crushed. Slowly pour in the peanut oil to form a thick pesto paste consistency.

Refrigerate for at least 2 hours before serving.

Roasted Eggplant and Lemongrass Dip
Makes 2 cups

This dish is so easy it has only three main ingredients. Slow roasting the eggplant intensifies the flavour. The lemongrass is a fantastic addition to the dish.

500 g eggplant (approximately 1-2, depending on size)
6 large cloves garlic, peeled
1½ cups of olive oil
30 g lemongrass
salt and pepper

Cut off the ends of the eggplants and slice in half longways. Place the eggplants in a shallow baking tray and add the garlic. Pour over ½ cup of the olive oil to coat.

Bake in a 160°C oven for approximately 45 minutes until the eggplants have turned brown and become tender. Remove from the pan and drain, retaining the oil.

Place the lemongrass in a food processor and pulse until well broken down. It is important that the lemongrass is properly ground or the finished dip will have a stringy texture.

Once the lemongrass is well blended, add the baked eggplant in the processor and pulse. Slowly pour in the rest of the oil and season with salt and pepper.

Refrigerate for at least 2 hours before serving.

Avocado and Toasted Pine Nut Salsa
Makes 1 cup

Remember guacamole? This is a new deli version of the familiar classic. Dice the avocado to add texture. Adjust the chilli to suit. Use only vine-ripened tomatoes: the alternatives just don't have enough flavour.

1 avocado, finely diced
½ clove garlic, finely diced
6 small vine-ripened tomatoes, diced
1 small red chilli, seeded and diced
juice of ½ a lemon
75 g toasted pine nuts
salt and pepper

Combine all the ingredients in a bowl. Stir until well combined. Refrigerate before serving.

Artichoke Salad

Serves 12 as an antipasto or 6 as an entrée

Fresh artichokes have a limited season so try this when they're available. The preparation is a bit involved but well worth it. (Marcella Hazan's instructions on how to prepare these tricky vegetables are the best I've come across yet. I've reproduced them here from her book *The Essentials of Classic Italian Cooking*, published by Knopf.) The marinade is a very simple and traditional Florentine recipe. Serve either as an antipasto or as a side dish. (Incidentally, during the Renaissance artichokes were considered a very powerful aphrodisiac!)

12 artichokes
1 lemon

pinch salt
2 bay leaves
½ a lemon

Dressing:
2 cloves garlic, finely chopped
salt and pepper
juice of 1½ lemons
1 tablespoon red wine vinegar
generous handful of freshly chopped basil and freshly chopped mint

To prepare the artichokes, discard all of the tough, inedible leaves and portions of leaves. Start by bending back the outer leaves, pulling them down towards the base. Do not take off the paler bottom end of the leaf because this point is tender and edible. As you take more leaves off and get deeper into the artichoke, the tender part at which the leaves will snap will be further and further from the base. Keep pulling off single leaves until you expose a central cone of leaves that are green only at the tip, and whose paler whitish base is at least 4 cm high. Once you have got to this stage, go back and carefully trim away any tough green part of the leaves that remains.

Slice at least 2.5 cm off the top of the central cone to get rid of the tough green part. Take half the lemon and rub the cut portions of the artichoke to prevent them from discolouring.

In the exposed centre of the artichoke at the bottom are small leaves with prickly tips curving inward. Cut off all the little leaves and scrape away the fuzzy 'choke' beneath them, being careful not to cut away any of the tender bottom. If you have a small knife with a rounded point, it will be easier to do this part of the trimming.

Turn the artichoke upside down and pare away the tough green layer of the stem all the way to the base of the artichoke, leaving the white part intact. Rub all exposed surfaces with the remaining half of the lemon.

Bring a pot of salted water to the boil. Add the artichokes, salt, bay leaves and lemon. Cook the artichokes until they are tender. Depending on their size, this takes between 20 and 40 minutes. Once tender, drain in a colander, refresh in iced water to retain colour and chill quickly.

Combine all the dressing ingredients. Pour over the artichokes and let rest for 2-3 hours before serving.

Pepperonata
Slow-Roasted Capsicums
Makes 8

This is always a deli favourite in summer. The addition of the anchovies and the balsamic vinegar intensifies the flavour produced by the slow roasting.

4 average-sized capsicums, halved (but leaving the stalk in place on each half), seeds and membranes removed.
6 anchovies
4 cloves garlic
1 teaspoon chopped rosemary
a little olive oil
12 vine-ripened tomatoes, quartered
2 tablespoons chopped basil
salt and pepper
splash of balsamic vinegar
olive oil

Sauté the anchovies, garlic and rosemary together in a little olive oil until the garlic is clear and tender. Then distribute the mixture evenly into the capsicum halves.

Combine and toss the other ingredients, then place in the prepared capsicum halves. Drizzle with a little olive oil and bake in a 150°C pre-heated oven for 1 hour.

Don't be put off by anchovies. They provide an amazing base to many sauces and dishes. They are also fantastic on an antipasto platter.

Grilled Calamari

Serves 4-6 as an entrée or can be divided evenly to top of each portion of the Black Squid Ink Risotto (p.36)

Calamari (squid) is such an underused food. Prepared well, it will take on any flavour you put with it. When buying squid, look for baby tubes or the smallest tubes available. If you find the tubes are too tough, marinate them in a little milk before putting into their final marinade.

4 squid tubes

Marinade:
1 clove garlic, crushed
4 kaffir lime leaves, thinly sliced
2 tablespoons fish sauce
juice of 1 lemon or 2 limes
1 tablespoon grapeseed oil
1 chilli, finely sliced

Clean the squid tubes by washing under cold water, removing the spine, any membrane and excess matter. Open them up and make criss-cross cuts along the top side of the tubes.

Combine all the marinade ingredients and marinate the squid for a minimum of 2 hours. Heat a grill pan or barbecue. Spray on a little oil and cook the squid for approximately 2-3 minutes on each side.

Roasted Leeks with Prosciutto and Salted Capers

Makes 8 bundles or serves 4 as an entrée

The subtle flavour of the leeks combined with the saltiness of the prosciutto and capers makes this an excellent dish. Serve as an antipasto dish or as an entrée with grilled bruschetta, or try it as a side dish with pork or chicken.

1 bay leaf
400 mls water
juice of 1 lemon
salt and pepper

1 leek, cleaned, trimmed and julienned

8 slices prosciutto
4 tablespoons olive oil
2 tablespoons salted capers, refreshed in warm water for 30 minutes
(to remove the external salt coating and soften the caper)
juice of ½ a lemon
a sprinkle of freshly ground pepper

Combine the bay leaf, water, lemon juice and salt and pepper and bring to a simmer. Add the leeks (keeping them straight) and cook until tender (approximately 3-4 minutes). Remove the leeks from the pan. Refresh in ice-cold water as this will help to retain their colour. Once chilled, remove leeks and drain all excess water.

Form the leeks into 8 bundles and wrap in prosciutto. Place on baking tray. Sprinkle with olive oil, capers, lemon juice and pepper. Grill for 5-7 minutes, turning twice, until slightly golden.

Roasted Garlic, Lemon and Saffron Risotto Balls Stuffed with Bocconcini

Makes 20 cocktail-sized balls or 8 large balls

Arancini (rice balls) are traditionally served as an antipasto, but with the sweetness of the roasted garlic and the richness of the saffron, they make a stunning lunch dish. You can make this recipe with any risotto, but I do recommend leaving it overnight before cooking as the resulting balls will be firmer. The addition of the bocconcini gives the balls a rich creamy centre once they are heated.

4 tablespoons olive oil
4 medium shallots, peeled and quartered
1 head of garlic, peeled and bashed
salt and pepper
2 sprigs of fresh oregano
2 cups arborio rice
500 mls chicken stock
1 cup white wine
juice of 2 lemons
rind of 1 lemon
1 teaspoon saffron, soaked in a little cold water for approximately 30 minutes
salt and pepper
½ cup freshly grated parmesan cheese
2 bocconcini balls, cut into quarters for the larger rice balls (or into smaller pieces for the smaller rice balls)
⅓ cup grapeseed oil for shallow frying

Heat the olive oil in a pan. Add the shallots and garlic. Season with salt and pepper. Add the fresh oregano. Toss. Transfer the pan to an oven and bake at 160°C for approximately 30 minutes. This gives a nice caramelised roast flavour to the shallots and garlic.

Separately sauté rice in a little oil, add the shallot mixture, then add to the mixture about 1 cup of the chicken stock, the wine, lemon juice, lemon rind and saffron. Stir and keep adding the stock gradually until it is all combined and all the liquid is absorbed (approximately 20 minutes). The rice should end up being creamy but still al dente.

Towards the end add the salt and pepper and parmesan cheese. Let the risotto cool overnight, then roll into balls about the size of a tennis ball (or smaller if making little balls for a party). Poke your finger into the middle of each ball and stuff a little piece of bocconcini into each one. Close the balls up and chill for at least 4 hours.

Shallow fry the balls in the grapeseed oil until the outsides are slightly browned. Then bake in a 180°C oven for 20 minutes until heated through, turning every so often so they do not burn.

Moroccan Stuffed Mussels
Stuffs approximately 30-35 green-lipped mussels

The combination of the parsley and coriander with the pickled lemon, chilli and spices is known in Morocco as chermoulla: it is to the Moroccans what pesto is to the Italians. It is worth mentioning that New Zealand's green-lipped mussels are much larger than their Australian or European counterparts. Serve these stuffed mussels as an entrée or as an antipasto.

1½ kg of live mussels, cleaned
½ cup water
½ cup dry white wine
½ a lemon, finely sliced

Stuffing:
1 fillet of white fish such as gurnard or similar, poached, cooled and flaked
1 preserved lemon, rinsed, flesh removed and the skin finely diced
3 teaspoons chopped fresh parsley
3 teaspoons chopped fresh coriander
1 small red chilli, finely chopped
½ teaspoon turmeric
½ teaspoon ground cumin
salt and pepper
2 tablespoons extra virgin light olive oil or grapeseed oil

In a large pot, place the cleaned mussels, water, dry white wine and lemon slices. Steam for 3-4 minutes until they are cooked and have opened. Discard any mussels that stay closed.

Combine the prepared fish with all the other stuffing ingredients to form a paste. (You can use a food processor for this step, but I recommend pulsing rather than blending.) Using a teaspoon, place a little stuffing in each of the mussels.

Stuffed Turkish Bread

When sliced, makes 8 pieces

A modern deli interpretation of garlic bread and so easy. The anchovies add a bit of a bite to the flavour. Try out a few other variations, for example caramelised onion and blue cheese or semi-dried tomato, feta and basil.

1 flat Turkish bread or similar Naan bread
1 onion, sliced
4 cloves garlic, crushed
1 cup grated edam cheese
½ cup grated parmesan cheese
4 anchovy fillets, quartered (optional)
salt and pepper
2 tablespoons olive oil

Lay the bread flat and layer half with the onion, garlic, cheeses and anchovies. Season with salt and pepper. Fold the top of the bread over. Brush the top with the olive oil. Place in a 180°C oven for 5 minutes until the top has slightly browned. Remove from the oven and cover with tin foil. Place back into the oven and cook for a further 15 minutes until the onion is tender.

Sweetcorn, Kaffir Lime and Tomato Salsa

Makes 1 cup

Salsas are a fantastic low-fat alternative to dips. This one combines the freshness of sweetcorn with the citrus tang of the lime leaves and juice. Use it as a dip or try it as a sauce for pan-fried fish or chicken.

1 cob of fresh sweetcorn
6 kaffir lime leaves, spine removed and finely shredded
4 small vine-ripened tomatoes, diced
juice of 1 lime
2 tablespoons chopped fresh basil
salt and pepper

Strip the corn cob by standing it upright on a board and slicing off the kernels. Combine the kernels with all the other ingredients in a bowl. Stir until everything is well combined. Refrigerate until well chilled before serving.

Romescue

Makes 1-1½ cups

Romescue is a traditional Eastern European sauce (originally made with ground almonds) used on fish. In this variation I have introduced smoked paprika, which adds a wonderful flavour.

16 small vine-ripened tomatoes
1 red capsicum, cut in half, seeds and membranes removed
4 cloves garlic, peeled
1 tablespoon olive oil
2 teaspoons Spanish smoked paprika (available from specialty food stores)
6 slices wholemeal bread, crusts removed and lightly toasted
salt and pepper

Place the tomatoes, capsicum and garlic in a shallow baking tray, sprinkle over the olive oil and bake in a moderate oven (approximately 180°C) for about 30 minutes. Remove and allow to cool.

Remove the skins from the tomatoes and the capsicum. Place the tomatoes, capsicum and garlic in a food processor and blend. Add the paprika. Break up the bread and add to the processor. Blend and season with salt and pepper.

Refrigerate for a minimum of 2 hours before serving.

pastas, pulses & grains

Pasta, pulses and grains are the staples of any kitchen. There's nothing simpler than a quickly assembled pasta dish when you've got friends coming over in 20 minutes.

Of the hundreds of types of pasta available in Italy, many have worked their way into our neck of the woods. If you're armed with just a few of these, plus one or two from a whole host of Asian noodle forms, a substantial meal is only moments away.

The humble bag of rice is a basic ingredient for people the world over. Cholesterol-, gluten- and fat-free, and an excellent source of complex carbohydrates, it is fundamental to the Asian diet and highly favoured for Italian risottos.

Beans were popular with the ancient Egyptians, and piles of them have been found in the tombs of the pharaohs, presumably to provide sustenance to the kings on their journey to the afterlife. With such illustrious beginnings, pulses have never really gone out of fashion. It's worth noting, though, that although canned beans can save tears at the end of a busy day

(and are a pantry must for this reason), dried beans really do provide superior results. You just need to soak them well before cooking. Cover them with water the night before or in the morning and they'll be ready to cook when you come home.

Versatility, adaptability and creativity are the keys to this section. I've introduced the yin and yang effect of sweet and sour combined with the heat of a little chilli. Find inspiration in the recipes for Spaghetti with Prosciutto, Lemon, Olives, Chilli and Mint (p.35) and the Warm Cannellini Bean Salad with Pepperoni, Garlic, Lemon and Mint (p.45).

These can be main meal dishes in their own right, but many of these recipes can be served as a side dish or a salad as well. Mix and match – it couldn't be easier.

Spaghetti with Prosciutto, Lemon, Olives, Chilli and Mint

Serves 4

Yet another traditional Italian dish, this is one of my all-time favourites. It's extremely easy to make with its olive oil base, but make sure you use only a very good quality extra virgin olive oil. The combination of garlic, chilli, olives and prosciutto is enhanced by the sharpness of the lemon and the sweetness of the mint. Top with freshly grated parmesan cheese. It's a real winner.

250 g spaghetti
150 mls extra virgin olive oil
4 cloves garlic, thinly sliced
1 red bird's-eye chilli, cut in half and seeded (add to taste)
125 g kalamata olives, pitted if desired
6 slices prosciutto, thinly sliced and torn into smaller pieces
juice of 2 lemons
3 tablespoons chopped mint
fresh parmesan cheese

Bring a large pot of salted water to the boil and cook the pasta according to the instructions on the packet.

Gently heat the olive oil in a large frying pan and add the garlic, chilli and olives. When the garlic has softened add the prosciutto and stir until slightly browned and a little crisp. Reduce heat and add the lemon juice.

Add the drained pasta and mint to the prosciutto mixture and toss through. Serve with shaved parmesan cheese.

Black Squid Ink Risotto with Baby Spinach
Serves 6

To dress this dish up for a dinner party, top with the Grilled Calamari (p.24) and some grilled black asparagus. (The latter is seasonal so can be a bit tricky to get, but it does make a beautiful addition.) Because of the richness of this risotto, with its squid ink, go easy on the parmesan cheese.

1 onion, diced
2 cloves garlic
2 tablespoons olive oil
2 cups arborio rice
1 cup wine
150 g white fish fillets, diced
500 mls fish stock
1 pouch squid ink (available from specialty food stores. Note it comes in a small pack, approximately 4 g and, if unopened, keeps indefinitely.)
salt and pepper
juice of ½ a lemon
1 good knob of butter
2 cups fresh baby spinach
½ cup chopped basil
⅓ cup parmesan cheese

Sauté the onion and garlic in a little olive oil until softened. Add the arborio rice and stir, coating all of the rice grains with the oil. The rice will make a slight popping noise.

Add the wine and deglaze the juices from the bottom of the pan by heating over a low element for a minute or so. Add the diced fish fillets, 1 cup of stock and the squid ink. Stir regularly until the stock is absorbed. Keep adding the stock and stirring until the rice has absorbed all the liquid and is creamy and al dente (approximately 20 minutes). Add a little water if more liquid is required. Season with salt, pepper and the lemon juice.

When the risotto is cooked fold through the butter, spinach, basil and parmesan cheese.

Japanese Udon Noodle Soup

Serves 4

Udon noodles are a traditional thick noodle that originated from Japan. I like their texture in this soup, but they can be substituted with any other noodle you prefer. This soup is a nice simple one and is very light and healthy. To make it into more of a meal, add the Roasted Duck Breast with Kaffir Lime, Star Anise and Sesame (p.62) or some grilled fish or chicken.

1 onion, finely sliced
4 cloves garlic, diced
1 stalk lemongrass, finely sliced
2 tablespoons grapeseed oil
1 carrot, finely sliced
2 sticks celery, finely sliced
1 red capsicum, finely sliced
500 mls chicken or vegetable stock
3 tablespoons sake or rice wine vinegar
3 tablespoons light soy sauce
2 cups prepared Asian greens, e.g. bok choy, spring onion
3 kaffir lime leaves, shredded
salt and pepper
approximately 400 g noodles (I use udon)

In a large saucepan, sauté the onion, garlic and lemongrass in the grapeseed oil. Add the sliced carrot, celery and capsicum and sauté for 3-5 minutes until lightly coated. Add the stock, sake (or vinegar) and the soy sauce and bring to the boil. Add the Asian greens and shredded lime leaves and season with salt and pepper.

Cook noodles as per instructions on the packet and add to the soup. If desired, garnish with bean sprouts and some chopped spring onion.

Asian Risotto
Serves 4

Risotto is a staple of the Italian diet and rice a staple of the Asian diet. So why not combine the two? I have used basmati rice but use arborio if you're more comfortable with it. I've made this dish vegetarian, because it will easily take on any flavour you could want to put with it. As a vegetarian dish it is also ideal to serve with any Asian-inspired main, such as the Grilled Calamari (p.24), or with the Roasted Duck Breast with Kaffir Lime, Star Anise and Sesame (p.62). Experiment with different stocks and try it with chicken or seafood.

When using fresh coriander roots, wash the roots and drain them well on paper towels. If you want to store them wrap in cling film. They will keep in your fridge for several days or can be frozen for longer. This is a very good way of giving a dish like this an intense coriander flavour.

4 cloves garlic, finely sliced
1 onion, finely sliced
1 tablespoon freshly chopped ginger
roots of 4 sprigs of coriander
2 sprigs of lemongrass
1 red chilli, seeded and chopped
2 tablespoons peanut oil
1½ cups basmati rice
1 cup dry white wine
1 red capsicum, membranes removed, seeded and cubed
500 mls vegetable stock
6 green beans, thinly sliced

½ cup chopped fresh Asian herbs (e.g. Vietnamese mint, basil and coriander)
2 tablespoons fish sauce
juice of 1 lemon
2 tablespoons kecap manis (an Asian sweet chilli sauce available from Asian supermarkets, assorted supermarkets and delis)

Sauté the garlic, onion, ginger, coriander root, lemongrass and chilli in the peanut oil. Add the rice and cook for about 1 minute, stirring so all the grains are well coated with the oil. Add the wine and the red capsicum, then the vegetable stock at regular intervals, stirring until all the liquid has been absorbed and the rice is al dente and creamy (approximately 20 minutes). Add the green beans and fold them through. Finish by adding the Asian herbs, fish sauce, lemon juice and kecap manis at the end.

Spaghetti with Slow Roasted Tomatoes, Mussels and Basil
Serves 4

We New Zealanders are so lucky to have our green-lipped mussels, which are far more flavoursome and luscious than their northern hemisphere equivalents. The key to this dish is the slow roasting of the tomatoes, which intensifies their flavour. Once this is done the rest of the recipe is simple and straightforward.

8 large (or 16 small) vine-ripened tomatoes, cut in halves
sprinkle of sea salt
freshly cracked pepper
olive oil
1 cup dry white wine
2 tablespoons olive oil
2 tablespoons butter
32 live mussels in the shell, cleaned
2 cloves garlic, crushed
250 g spaghetti, cooked and drained
fresh basil, chopped

Place the tomatoes in a baking tray. Season with the salt and pepper and drizzle with olive oil. Roast at 150°C for 1 hour. Remove the tomatoes from the tray. Allow them to cool a little before removing their skins. Deglaze the tray by adding a little of the wine to the pan and heating over a low heat for a minute or so. Reserve the liquid and tomatoes. Keep warm.

Heat the oil and butter in a deep pan. Add the mussels, cover the pan and shake for approximately 1-2 minutes until they are coated. Add the prepared tomatoes and their cooking liquid, garlic and the remaining wine and cook until the mussels have opened. (Discard any that do not open properly.) Toss the basil through the mixture.

Divide the pasta between 4 bowls and top with the mussel sauce. Serve with grilled bruschetta.

Sea salt is now quite commonly available and can be bought at supermarkets and specialty food stores. It has a much more intense flavour than regular table salt. Yes, it does cost more but you use much less. Buy whole peppercorns and crush them in a peppermill or mortar and pestle. There is nothing like freshly cracked pepper for instant flavour.

Puy Lentil Broth with Smoked Tuna and Broad Beans
Serves 4

This broth is a meal in itself. Puy lentils are a nice dark green colour and have a rich earthy flavour. Once cooked they hold their shape well, unlike many other pulses. Their flavour in this broth is enhanced by the smokiness of the fish and paprika.

1 onion, diced
4 cloves garlic, diced
2 tablespoons olive oil
300 g puy lentils
1 large carrot, diced
2 courgettes, sliced
750 mls fish stock
250 g smoked tuna, diced
1 teaspoon smoked paprika
juice of 1 lemon
2 teaspoons chopped fresh thyme
1 cup cooked, shelled broad beans

Sauté the onion and garlic in the olive oil until tender, then add the lentils and sauté until well coated. Add the carrot, courgettes and stock. Bring to a simmer and add the diced smoked tuna, paprika, lemon juice and fresh thyme and cook until the lentils are tender (approximately 20-25 minutes). Add the cooked broad beans at the end and fold through (this way they retain their colour and freshness).

Warm Cannellini Bean Salad with Pepperoni, Garlic, Lemon and Mint

Serves 4

This is a wonderful stand-by for a cold winter night, served with grilled bruschetta and a glass of riesling. It can also be served cold as a salad.

3 tablespoons olive oil
1 onion, finely sliced
6 cloves garlic
1 pepperoni stick, sliced diagonally
2 x 400 g tins whole peeled Italian tomatoes (crush them by hand to give the desired texture)
½ cup dry white wine
400 g dried cannellini beans soaked overnight, boiled until al dente (or substitute with 2 tins of drained, rinsed canned beans)
⅓ cup chopped mint
juice of 2 lemons
salt and pepper

Heat the oil in a heavy-based pan, then add the onion and garlic and sauté until the onion is translucent and the garlic is tender. Add the pepperoni and sauté until it has been well browned on all sides. Add the tomatoes and the wine.

Bring to the boil, reduce the temperature and simmer uncovered for approximately 20 minutes until the sauce has thickened and most of the liquid has evaporated. Add the cannellini beans, mint and lemon juice and season with salt and pepper.

Canelloni with Tomato Sauce and Handmade Ricotta Cheese
Serves 6

This recipe requires a little effort, but the end result is definitely worth it. The handmade ricotta can be substituted with store-bought ricotta or cottage cheese. Serve with a crisp green salad.

18 cannelloni tubes

Basic Tomato Sauce (p.53 note, however, that for this recipe the sauce should be made with 3 tins of whole peeled tomatoes, not 2.)

Stuffing:
1 small onion, finely diced
a little olive oil
1 heaped teaspoon of salted capers, refreshed in cold water for approximately 30 minutes, then drained and finely chopped
2 cups handmade ricotta cheese (p.93) or cottage cheese (well drained)
1 cup shredded mozzarella cheese
½ cup grated parmesan cheese
250 g (approx.) spinach, cleaned, steamed, fully drained and chopped (or 2 pre-packaged bags, available at the supermarket),
pinch of dried oregano
½ teaspoon grated nutmeg
handful of chopped basil

Sauté the onion in the oil.

In a separate bowl, combine the capers, 3 cheeses, spinach, dried oregano, nutmeg and basil. Then add the softened onion and mix well.

Cook the cannelloni tubes if necessary according to the packet instructions. Stuff the tubes with the cheese mixture.

Layer approximately a third of the sauce in the bottom of a baking pan with sides. Place the stuffed tubes on top of the sauce. Distribute remaining sauce over the top of the tubes. Cover with fresh grated parmesan. Cover with tin foil and bake at 170°C for approximately 25 minutes. Remove the tin foil and cook for a further 5 minutes until the cheese on top is golden.

mains

Maximum flavour is the key here. I've used a number of herbs and spices that may not be standard in most kitchens, but these can be easily found in any Asian foodstore. I'm also a great believer in organic produce and meats and encourage you to use them as they do provide a truly superior flavour. This chapter includes recipes that can be used for brunches, lunches, picnics, entrées and dinners.

ere in New Zealand we're surrounded by plentiful seas and we've also developed leaner cuts of meat that are appreciated the world over. Good farming practice means our flocks and herds are free from diseases that plague other countries. Specialty meats, too, have made their way to our shores and into our recipes. Once something of a rarity, duck now appears regularly on the menus of many of New Zealand's top restaurants and delicatessens.

I'm a great believer in organic meat and poultry, using them whenever I can. I encourage you to do the same as they provide a truly superior flavour. Also, always check the freshness of the produce that you buy to ensure that it's of the highest quality. Build a good relationship with your local butcher: the meat is most often very fresh and the staff has a wealth of knowledge about cuts and suitable alternatives.

Maximum flavour is the key in this section. The Basic Tomato Sauce recipe (p.53) has a

wonderful intensity that can be used in a number of dishes. It is great to have on hand, so make it in bulk and freeze it into handy portions. I've used a number of herbs and spices that may not be standard in most kitchens but are easily found in Asian foodstores. Look for the plants themselves and try them out in your garden. Star anise is an aromatic spice native to China and kaffir lime leaves are an essential of Southeast Asian cuisine. Although now grown in New Zealand, kaffir lime leaves are seasonal, so when you find them, freeze them. Otherwise, you can buy dried leaves from Asian supermarkets. Kecap manis is a thick brown sweet soy sauce from Indonesia. I've used it with sweet chilli on salmon, but also try it mixed with lime juice as a marinade for chicken.

This chapter includes recipes that can be used for brunches, lunches, entrées and dinners. Dishes such as the salmon fillet and the beef eye fillet can be served whole for party foods, or adapted to suit smaller, more informal dinners.

Herbs

Wherever you can use fresh herbs. I recommend a comprehensive herb garden, but most of the traditional herbs are now readily available in supermarkets. If the more exotic ones, such as kaffir lime leaves and lemongrass, are a bit scarce, when you do find them, buy in bulk and freeze them. Note that dried kaffir lime leaves are available in Asian supermarkets. If you can't find Thai basil and Vietnamese mint it's quite acceptable to substitute them with the more traditional varieties.

Basic Tomato Sauce

Makes 2½-3 cups
This very traditional tomato sauce as used by early pizza makers from Naples has only a few ingredients. Don't let the anchovies put you off: they give the sauce a body that can't be equalled. When choosing whole peeled tomatoes, select ones that are plump, ripe and in a thick juice. Oregano is one of the few dried herbs that I would recommend using. Use this sauce on pizza and pasta and feel free to add your own personal touches.

4 cloves garlic, chopped finely
4 tablespoons extra virgin olive oil
4 anchovy fillets
2 x 400 g tins whole peeled Italian tomatoes
½ teaspoon dried oregano
½ cup dry white wine
salt and pepper

Sauté the garlic in oil. Add the anchovies, sauté and break up into a paste. Add the tomatoes (crush them by hand to give the desired texture), dried oregano and wine.

Simmer uncovered for approximately 20-30 minutes to reduce this to a thick sauce. Add salt and pepper to taste.

Harissa-Crusted Eye Fillet Steak with Gremolata
Serves 8-10

Nothing looks more impressive than an eye fillet steak cooking away on a barbecue. Harissa is a traditional salty chilli spice from Morocco. With the addition of the sugar it caramelises the marinade onto the meat. The smell as it's cooking is sure to win you points with your friends. The gremolata, a traditional Italian citrus and garlic seasoning, is a perfect fresh finish to this dish.

1 whole eye fillet steak, trimmed weight approximately 1.5 kg

Harissa marinade:
1 teaspoon black peppercorns
1 teaspoon cardamom seeds
2 teaspoons coriander seeds
4 large red chillies, seeded and finely chopped
4 large cloves of garlic, crushed
2 tablespoons salt
2 tablespoons sugar
juice of 1 lemon
2 tablespoons olive oil

Gremolata:
2 cloves garlic, finely chopped
rind of 2 lemons, finely chopped
2 tablespoons finely chopped Italian flat leaf parsley

Crush the black peppercorns, cardamom and coriander seeds with a mortar and pestle. Combine with all the other harissa ingredients and coat the steak. Refrigerate, covered, for several hours.

Remove from the fridge and bring up to room temperature before barbecuing.

To cook, place the steak over a hot grill plate, turning every few minutes, so as to sear the whole fillet. Continue to cook, turning the meat every so often so that the whole fillet cooks evenly. For rare to medium cook for approximately 20-25 minutes (depending upon the size of the fillet).

Allow to stand a further 15 minutes before slicing. Top with the gremolata, which is made by combining the garlic, lemon rind and parsley.

Muffuletta
Cut loaf serves 6

This traditional New Orleans lunch dish is basically a stuffed loaf of bread. This recipe offers just one suggestion for this simple, delicious sandwich: lots of different fillings are possible. Tie the stuffed roll with string and weigh it down by stacking plates on top of it. You can make this either as a full roll or cut into individual sandwiches to take on a picnic.

1 large ciabatta loaf (if you can't get ciabatta, try a cob or something similar)
6 thin slices prosciutto
a handful of spinach leaves or other salad greens (enough to provide a thin layer across the loaf)
approximately 2 tablespoons olive tapenade
2 tomatoes, finely sliced
approximately 4 bocconcini balls, thinly sliced
4 artichoke hearts, thinly sliced
6 good-sized leaves of fresh basil, roughly chopped
olive oil
salt and pepper
squeeze of lemon juice (optional)

Cut open the loaf lengthwise and drizzle a little olive oil on the base. Layer all the ingredients on top of each other inside. Dress with olive oil, season with salt and pepper and a squeeze of lemon juice (optional). Tie the loaf with string and place on a plate. Weigh the loaf down with heavy plates on top for approximately 3-4 hours before serving.

Oven-Baked Salmon Fillet with Japanese Salad

Serves 8-10 or 16-18 for a party

Because it is so versatile, easy to prepare and readily available, I've developed several new ways of preparing sides of fresh New Zealand salmon. This recipe uses the flavours of Japan, with the wasabi and lemon bringing out the richness of the fish. Garnished with the Japanese salad it makes a beautiful dish.

1 side fresh salmon, boned

Marinade:
2 tablespoons wasabi paste
1 tablespoon sesame oil
juice of 1 lemon

Japanese salad:
1 red capsicum, seeds and membrane removed
½ cucumber, peeled and seeded
½ cup bean sprouts
½ cup of spring onion greens, finely sliced on the diagonal
1 cm piece fresh ginger, shredded

Dressing:
50 mls Japanese rice wine vinegar or sake
75 mls Japanese soy sauce
50 mls sesame oil
juice of ½ a lemon
1 clove garlic, crushed

Garnish:
1 sheet of nori, cut in quarters and finely sliced using scissors
1 teaspoon black sesame seeds

Place the salmon on a greased baking sheet. Whisk the wasabi paste, sesame oil and lemon juice together until it becomes a slightly creamy marinade. Rub into the salmon and let stand for 30 minutes.

Julienne the red capsicum and cucumber, and toss together with the bean sprouts, spring onion greens and shredded ginger.

Combine all the dressing ingredients and toss together. Mix the dressing through the salad.

Bake the salmon at 180°C for 7-9 minutes for rare, 13-15 minutes for well done. Cooking times will vary depending upon the size and thickness of the salmon. Remove from the oven and allow to cool. Place the salmon on a serving platter, top with the salad and garnish with the nori and black sesame seeds.

Asian Roasted Chicken
Serves 4-6

This variation on traditional stuffed chicken has a mild but very refreshing flavour. Alter the combination of garlic and lemon to suit your own palate.

1 whole organic chicken (approximately 1.5 kg)

Stuffing:
2 cm piece of ginger, peeled and bashed
1 head of garlic, peeled and bashed
1 stalk of lemon grass, bashed
2 lemons cut into halves
4 bird's-eye chillies cut into halves
8 kaffir lime leaves, torn

Marinade:
juice of 1 lemon
2 tablespoons fish sauce
2 tablespoons sesame oil
salt and pepper to taste

Mix stuffing ingredients together. Stuff the bird with the mixture and close up the cavity using a skewer or by tying the ends of the legs together with cotton string. Baste with the marinade. Place the bird into a roasting pan breast side down. Add 1 cup of water.

Roast in a pre-heated 180°C oven for 30 minutes. Turn the bird over and roast for a further 30 minutes. Make sure that the chicken is thoroughly cooked by inserting a knife between the breast and the leg: any juices should run clear. Season with salt and pepper to taste.

Around for centuries but recently made famous by a popular British chef, the mortar and pestle is a tool I use all the time. Use it for crushing herbs and spices. Look for heavy, solid stone mortar and pestles as they are far more efficient than the smaller ceramic ones.

Salmon and Potato Hash Cakes $6.95

Mushroom Risotto Cakes $6.95

Rosemary Basted Chicken Breast $6.95

Eggplant and feta frittata $6.95

Bacon and egg pie $6.95

Ham, zucchini and sundried tomato quiche $6.95

Potato Salad with Cream, zucchini

Roasted Duck Breast with Kaffir Lime, Star Anise and Sesame

Serves 4

The aromatic spices of the East wonderfully enhance the richness of duck. Either seared and baked in the oven or barbecued over a high heat, this dish is great as a main or sliced and used in a noodle salad (p.87) or a traditional Japanese raman or soup.

4 duck breasts, cleaned and trimmed leaving the skin on

Marinade:
12 kaffir lime leaves, shredded
1 cm piece of ginger, shredded
4 star anise, crushed
100 mls toasted sesame oil
juice of 2 limes
1 large clove of garlic, crushed

Place the duck breasts skin side up and slice each one diagonally approximately 4 times. (Cut through the skin but not the flesh.)

Combine all the ingredients for the marinade and pour over the duck. Marinate for 1-4 hours.

Oven baked:
For oven baking, place the duck skin side down in a shallow frypan in a 220°C oven for approximately 10-15 minutes. Then transfer the duck to an ovenproof dish and cook for another 7-10 minutes.

Barbecue:
To chargrill or barbecue, place the duck skin side down on a barbecue hot plate over a medium heat for approximately 10-15 minutes. Then turn over and cook for another 5 minutes.

In both cases let the duck stand for 5 minutes before serving.

Rolled Chicken Breasts with Spinach, Basil and Cheese

Serves 4

Use either the Handmade Ricotta (p.93 – or bought ricotta if that's easier) or bocconcini to stuff these chicken breasts. Serve with Roasted Vegetable Salad (p.76) and some garlic and rosemary roasted potatoes.

4 chicken breasts, skin off
spinach (enough to coat each open chicken breast, approximately two medium leaves per breast)
fresh basil (a couple of leaves per breast)
bocconcini, 1 ball cut in half per breast or 2 teaspoons ricotta cheese per breast
flour
olive oil, enough to lightly shallow fry
2 cups Basic Tomato Sauce (p.53)
2 tablespoons black kalamata olives, pitted if desired
2 tablespoons caperberries
½ cup white wine

Flatten the chicken breasts and layer the fresh spinach and basil leaves on top. Add either the bocconcini or ricotta. Roll up the breasts and secure with either a toothpick or a skewer. Coat with a little flour and brown in a little olive oil. Add to the pan the tomato sauce, olives, caperberries and wine.

Bake at 180°C for approximately 20-25 minutes until the chicken is cooked through and the sauce is reduced. Turn the chicken 2-3 times during the cooking process.

Porcini Tart

Makes 1 large 28 cm tart (cut into 8) or 6 individual tarts. If making individual tarts I would recommend using filo pastry.

This tart is a real deli classic. Porcini are traditional dried Italian mushrooms and can easily be found in specialty food stores. Much fuller in flavour than fresh mushrooms, porcini add an extraordinary richness to this dish.

Pastry:
1 cup of flour
50 g butter
pinch of salt
approximately 100 mls cold water

Filling:
60 g dried porcini mushrooms
100 g butter
2 tablespoons olive oil
1 onion, finely diced
500 g button mushrooms, quartered
½ cup chopped Italian flat leaf parsley
½ teaspoon chopped fresh rosemary
1 teaspoon fresh thyme
2 tablespoons tomato paste
salt and pepper
6 eggs
1 cup grated parmesan cheese

For the pastry, place the flour, butter and salt in a food processor and pulse until everything is combined. Slowly add the water, pulsing until it forms a tight ball. Remove the dough and knead on a lightly floured board until everything is well combined. Cover with cling film and place in the refrigerator for 30 minutes. Remove and roll out.

Place the pastry into a 28 cm tart pan with a removable base and gently press into place. Cover with tin foil and baking beans and bake blind at 180°C for 35-45 minutes until slightly browned.

If making individual tarts, for each tart cut 2 sheets of filo pastry into thirds lengthwise. Lightly grease a buffalo muffin tin with a little melted butter. Press in the filo, 1 sheet at a time, working around the muffin cup, buttering the filo as you go. Repeat for each of the six muffin cups. No need to pre-bake these as the cooking at the end is sufficient.

For the filling, soak the porcini in 1½ cups warm water for 30 minutes. Place the butter and oil into a pan, add the onions and button mushrooms and sauté. Drain the porcini, reserving the liquid. Add the porcini to the pan, along with the herbs, tomato paste and salt and pepper. Combine. Add the porcini stock and simmer until most of the liquid has evaporated.

Meanwhile combine the eggs and the parmesan. Allow the porcini mixture to cool before mixing through the egg mixture. Pour into the pre-cooked pastry shell and bake at 180°C for 30 minutes. If making individual tarts cook at 180°C for approximately 15-20 minutes.

Baked Salmon Fillet with Sweet Chilli and Kecap Manis
Serves 8-10

The salmon in this incredibly quick and easy recipe can be either baked as a whole side or portioned and grilled on the barbecue. It is fantastic served on a bed of Chargrilled Summer Vegetables (p.83) and topped with either freshly chopped coriander or Vietnamese mint.

1 side of fresh salmon, boned
4 tablespoons sweet chilli sauce
4 tablespoons kecap manis
juice of 1 lemon
2 tablespoons chopped coriander or Vietnamese mint

Combine the sweet chilli sauce, kecap manis and lemon juice and spoon over the salmon.

Oven baked:
For oven baking, I recommend you use a whole salmon side. Place the salmon on a greased baking sheet, skin side down, and bake at 180°C for 7-9 minutes for rare, 13-15 minutes for well done.

Barbecue:
To chargrill or barbecue, cut the salmon into portions (approximately 2 cm wide), place the salmon skin side down on a barbecue hot plate to sear the base, then turn over onto the grill to achieve the blackened line effect and cook for approximately 5-7 minutes.

To serve, place the salmon on a platter and garnish with the chopped coriander or mint.

Chicken Drumsticks Stuffed with Pine Nuts, Basil and Sultanas

Makes 4-6 drumsticks depending on size

These drumsticks are ideal for lunch or cold, taken on a picnic. The sweetness of the sultanas and the basil and the nuttiness of the pine nuts work well with the chicken.

Stuffing:
2 tablespoons toasted pine nuts
2 tablespoons sultanas, refreshed in warm water for approximately 30 minutes so they soften and plump up, then drained
½ tablespoon freshly chopped basil
½ teaspoon fresh nutmeg
salt and pepper
1 tablespoon olive oil

4-6 chicken drumsticks, skin on

Combine the pine nuts, sultanas, basil, nutmeg, salt and pepper and olive oil until well mixed.

Place your thumb under the chicken skin, pull back and use a teaspoon to stuff the prepared mixture into the cavity. Pull the skin back up, then secure with a toothpick. Bake in a moderate oven (160°C) for approximately 25 minutes, browning on all sides.

Citrus press
I use a lot of lemon and lime juice in my cooking, so a good press is really important. Life is too short to spend time squeezing by hand.

Whole peeled tomatoes
These are an essential in any pantry. When choosing, buy only Italian as these have the best flavour. Look for tomatoes that are well ripened and do not have woody ends, and are packed in a reasonably thick juice rather than a watery one. Surprisingly, often the best you'll find are the cheapest ones in your supermarket.

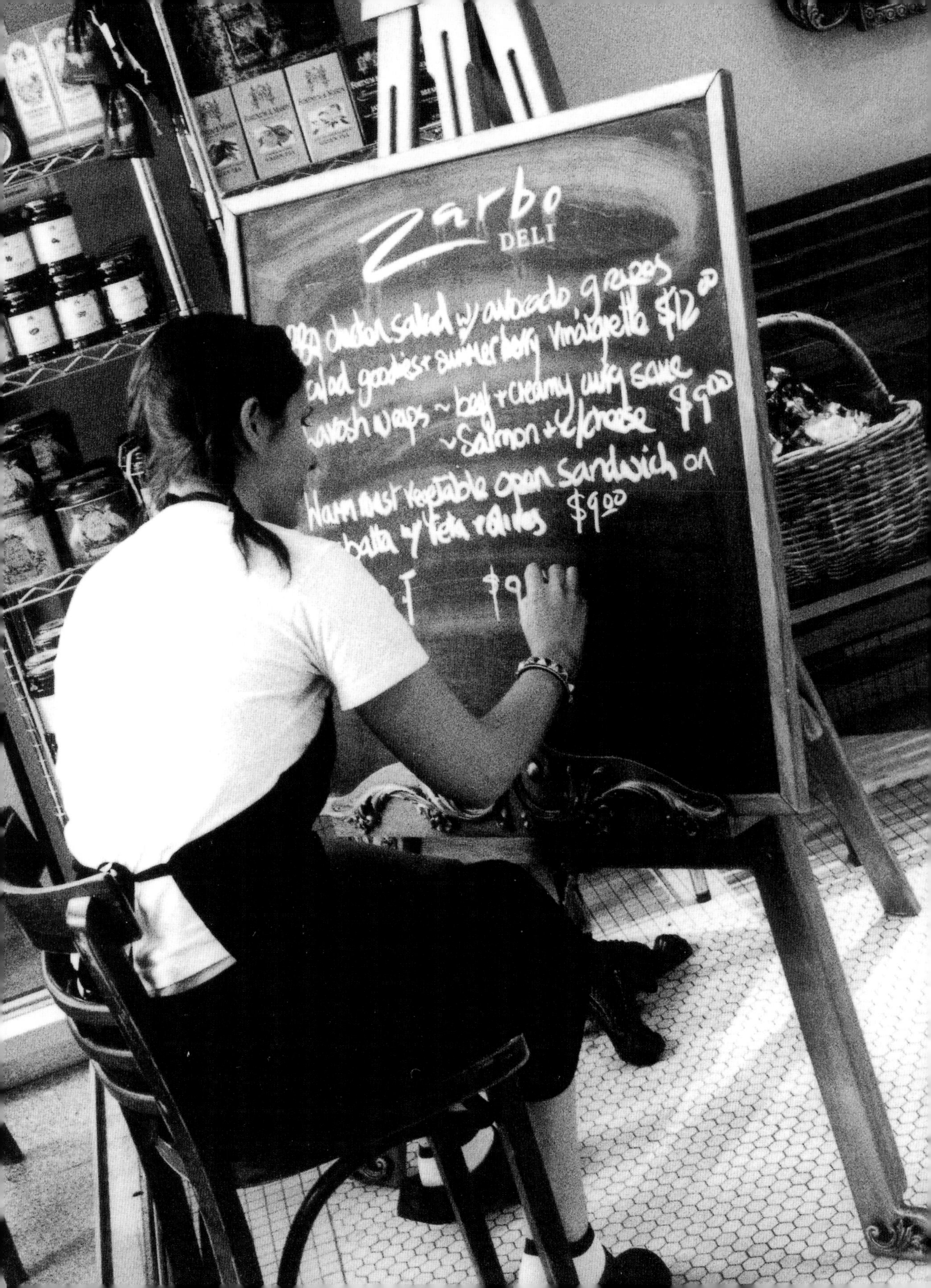

Zarbo
DELI
open sandwich on
$9.00

salads

Salads are a fundamental staple of any good deli. But at home there's no need to suffer uninspiring bowls of wilted lettuce and bland tomatoes: salads are limited only by your imagination. Freshness, colour and texture are vital. Adding fresh herbs or some well-chosen spices can do wonders.

othouse technology and deep refrigeration allow us to find favourite fruits and vegetables all year round. Some produce, however, is definitely seasonal and just tastes better when its turn genuinely comes around. A tomato becomes a delight when you're presented with the genuine vine-ripened version. Follow the seasons and look for interesting variations on the standard vegetables. Black asparagus, for example, can really add flair to a dish.

Overseas influences have had a great broadening effect on New Zealand cooking. Once unknown, couscous and orzo pasta now make their way to our tables on a regular basis. Don't be afraid to experiment and combine interesting ingredients – many of these are great in salads.

Dressings should be light and flavoursome, without being overbearing. Remember that green salads should be dressed only at the table, not left to languish in a pond of liquid at the bottom of the bowl. But salads that use ingredients such as pasta and grains should be dressed and allowed to stand in the refrigerator for a couple of hours before serving. This allows all the flavours to be absorbed. (But remember to re-toss before serving.)

Salads are an essential part of any barbecue, but don't think of them purely as a summer thing. You can chargrill vegetables all year round and combine them with chargrilled meats and seafoods. Salads are wonderfully versatile and can be just the thing to pad out a meal when you've got lots of mouths to feed, or as the main course when there are only a few of you. Anything goes.

Knives

If you're serious about cooking I do recommend investing in a good set of knives. They don't come cheaply, but good ones, well looked after, will last you a lifetime. I suggest a cook's knife somewhere between 19-24 cm, depending on personal preference; a filleting knife; a paring knife for those little jobs; and a decent bread knife. You will also need a steel for sharpening. Store knives in a knife block and never put them into the dishwasher.

Pawpaw and Prosciutto Salad
Serves 6

This simple, stunning combination makes a brilliant entrée. It needs to be assembled at the time of serving. Vietnamese mint is relatively difficult to procure, so if you can't get it substitute Thai basil or mint.

1 pawpaw, seeded, peeled and sliced
6 thin slices of prosciutto, torn lengthways into 3-4 strips

Dressing:
juice of 2 small limes
3 tablespoons very good quality olive oil
a very small pinch of sea salt
Vietnamese mint (or Thai basil or regular basil)

Arrange the pawpaw and prosciutto on a platter.

Whisk all other ingredients together until the mixture becomes slightly milky and starts to thicken. Pour over the salad. Top with chopped Vietnamese mint or basil.

Asian Lamb Salad
Serves 6

Lamb is an ideal meat to use with the ingredients in this marinade. I use grapeseed oil whenever I need an alternative to olive oil. It has similar health benefits and no real flavour. This salad is suitable for a light dinner.

8 lamb fillets

Marinade:
1 clove of garlic, chopped
2 cm piece of lemongrass, crushed and diced
1 cm piece of ginger, grated

1 tablespoon fish sauce
1 tablespoon kecap manis
splash of grapeseed oil

Dressing:
juice of 1 lime
rind of 1 lemon
2 tablespoons fish sauce
1 bird's-eye chilli, seeded and finely sliced
1 teaspoon grated palm sugar
1 tablespoon Kikkoman soy sauce

3-4 cups mesclun leaves
approximately 1 cup bean sprouts

Combine all marinade ingredients and marinate lamb fillets in a non-absorbent bowl for 2 hours, turning 2-3 times.

Combine all dressing ingredients and allow to stand.

Assemble the salad of mesclun salad leaves and bean sprouts.

Grill the lamb fillets and allow to stand for 10 minutes before slicing. Place the lamb over the salad leaves and spoon over the dressing.

Orzo Salad with Feta, Caperberries, Broad Beans and Italian Dressing
Serves 6-8

Orzo is a small rice-shaped grain-like pasta, originating from Greece, but also common throughout Italy. It can be used in a variety of salads. This one is very quick to prepare and full of flavour. You can use orzo in a warm salad to accompany a chicken- or tomato-based dish. Also try it in soups such as minestrone or in pasta dishes for children.

1½ cups of orzo pasta
1 teaspoon olive oil

Dressing:
60 mls red wine vinegar
20 mls balsamic vinegar
½ clove garlic, finely diced
1 teaspoon finely chopped fresh rosemary
2 teaspoons tomato paste

1 cup diced feta
2 cups broad beans, blanched and skins removed
½ cup caperberries, halved
½ cups cherry tomatoes, halved
½ cup chopped flat leaf Italian parsley

Cook orzo pasta in boiling salted water (to which 1 teaspoon of olive oil has been added) for approximately 7-10 minutes or until al dente. Stir occasionally to prevent the pasta sticking together.

Place all the dressing ingredients in a small bowl and stir until combined.

Drain the orzo to remove all excess water and cool. Place the orzo in a large bowl and add the feta, beans, caperberries, tomatoes and parsley. Add the dressing and toss until well combined.

Roasted Vegetable Salad with Citrus Paprikaed Snapper

Serves 4

This quick and easy dish is ideal for a warm summer evening. Use only Spanish smoked paprika. (Other paprikas provide colour only, but not the flavour.) Grill the vegetables first and allow them to cool a little before assembling the salad. The citrus and smokiness of the paprika work beautifully with the snapper, but other firm white-fleshed fish can be substituted if snapper (called bream in Australia) isn't available.

This is a very simple dish to make. The vegetables can be prepared earlier in the day and the fish then cooked to order and the dish assembled on a plate before serving.

Salad:
1 medium red capsicum, seeds and membranes removed, sliced
1 medium orange capsicum, seeds and membranes removed, sliced
1 Japanese eggplant, sliced diagonally
2 courgettes, sliced
2 cloves garlic, crushed
5 tablespoons olive oil
approximately 75 g mesclun lettuce

Marinade:
2 tablespoons lemon oil (available from specialty food stores and supermarkets)
juice of 1 lime
2 teaspoons Spanish smoked paprika (available from specialty food stores)
salt and pepper

Approximately 2 large fillets of snapper (or any other firm white fish), cut into 3-4 cm chunks

Dressing:
1 tablespoon olive oil
40 mls balsamic vinegar
1 tablespoon freshly chopped herbs (basil or chervil or similar)

Toss together all the salad ingredients except for the mesclun. Chargrill and then allow them to cool.

Combine all the marinade ingredients to form a paste and coat the fish. Marinate for a minimum of 30 minutes. Chargrill the fish and allow to cool.

To assemble, layer the mesclun with the vegetables and top with the fish. Combine all the dressing ingredients and pour over the salad.

Chinese Duck Coleslaw
Serves 4

You can use either the Roasted
Duck Breast with Kaffir Lime, Star
Anise and Sesame (p.62) or buy a
roasted duck from an Asian
market, which is what I do. If
duck is unavailable, substitute
chicken. The Asian dressing is a
spicy, healthy alternative to the
heavy, gluggy dressing that we're
traditionally used to in coleslaws.

Dressing:
6 star anise, crushed
20 mls fish sauce
80 mls sesame oil
20 mls kecap manis
salt and pepper

1 bird's-eye chilli, chopped
2 teaspoons grated fresh ginger

Salad:
⅓ cabbage, shredded
1 red capsicum, membranes and
seeds removed and sliced
1 cup bean sprouts
2 spring onions, sliced
meat of half a roasted duck
(cooked duck as purchased from
an Asian supermarket)
handful of chopped mint and
coriander

Combine all dressing ingredients.
Toss all the salad ingredients to
combine and fold through the
dressing.

A monoplane is one of the best kitchen tools I have bought in a long time. It grates the rind of lemons and limes and it's fantastic for shredding vegetables, garlic, ginger and lemongrass. I also use it for grating nutmeg, parmesan cheese, palm sugar, etc.

Israeli Couscous Salad with Cherry Tomatoes and Spanish Smoked Paprika
Serves 6

Israeli couscous is a grain-like ball much larger than traditional couscous and is available in specialty food stores. Once cooked it gives a sweet, nutty flavour. If it's unavailable use orzo instead.

a little olive oil
1 medium onion, finely diced
250 g Israeli couscous
salt and pepper

Salad:
1 cup sweet cherry tomatoes, cut into halves
3 red capsicums, seeded and de-membraned, charred, peeled and roughly sliced
⅓ cup chopped Italian flat leaf parsley

Dressing:
⅓ cup olive oil
¼ cup lemon juice
1 tablespoon Spanish smoked paprika (available from specialty food stores)
½ clove garlic, crushed
salt and pepper

To cook the Israeli couscous, heat a little oil in a heavy-based saucepan, add the onion and sauté until translucent. Then add the couscous and brown on all sides to seal. Season with salt and pepper and add boiling water to cover. Add one more cup of water, then cover the pot and simmer for 8-10 minutes, stirring once or twice during the cooking process. Drain in cold water.

Combine all the salad ingredients and set aside.

Make the dressing, pour over the salad and toss. Refrigerate for a few hours before serving, tossing every so often.

Chargrilled Summer Vegetables
Serves 6

In summer we have an abundance of fresh vegetables and this salad is a fantastic way to use them. The addition of the olive oil, balsamic vinegar and the fresh rustic herbs adds an unbeatable dimension. Grill in small batches, and serve either hot or at room temperature. Try variations of vegetables to make this an all-year-round dish.

1 eggplant, halved and sliced
3 capsicums, assorted colours, cut into halves, membranes and seeds removed and sliced into thirds
2 courgettes, sliced diagonally
150 g green beans
any other selected vegetables suitable for chargrilling (e.g. pumpkin, garlic, red onions or whatever else might be in your fridge)

½ cup olive oil (the eggplant soaks up a lot of oil)
3 tablespoons balsamic vinegar
3 teaspoons chopped garlic
1 teaspoon chopped rosemary
1 teaspoon chopped sage
sea salt and cracked pepper to taste

2 tablespoons balsamic vinegar
a little chopped fresh basil

Place all the vegetables in a large bowl and add the oil, vinegar, herbs, salt and pepper. Combine well and allow to stand. You may need to add more oil depending on how much the eggplant soaks up. (Don't add too much, though, or when the vegetables are grilled the excess oil will create a black smoke that spoils the flavour.)

Grill the vegetables in small batches over a hot barbecue. Toss well. Fold through 2 tablespoons of balsamic vinegar and a little chopped fresh basil before serving.

Quinoa with Roasted Pumpkin and Semi-Dried Tomato Salad

Serves 6-8

Pronounced 'keen-wah', quinoa, once a crucial ingredient for the ancient Incas, is today a much underused grain. Considered a complete protein by many dieticians, it contains all the essential amino acids and is higher in unsaturated fats (the good ones!) and lower in carbohydrates than most other grains. Like several of the other ingredients in this salad, quinoa can be found in most specialty food stores.

500 g quinoa

Salad:
1 eggplant, thinly sliced, oiled and chargrilled
2 courgettes, thinly sliced
1 block haloumi cheese (a traditional Turkish cheese, available from most supermarkets)
½ cup semi-dried tomatoes (available from delicatessens and specialty food stores. If unavailable, substitute with sun-dried tomatoes)
approximately 2 cups diced, roasted pumpkin

Dressing:
1 clove garlic, finely diced
1 tablespoon chopped fresh oregano or marjoram
pinch of salt and pepper
⅓ cup olive oil
40 mls red wine vinegar

Cook the quinoa in boiling, salted water for approximately 7 minutes and strain through a fine strainer. Note that once it is cooked, the grains are still small.

Slice the haloumi cheese into 8-10 thin slices and place under grill for a few minutes to brown slightly, or brown in a frypan in a little bit of oil. Then drain on absorbent paper. This process adds a lovely nutty flavour to the dish.

Combine the prepared eggplant, courgettes, haloumi cheese, tomatoes and pumpkin and add to the cooked quinoa.

Whisk all the dressing ingredients together and pour over the salad. Allow to stand for 2 hours before tossing and serving.

Nicoise Salad with Grilled Pancetta
Serves 4

The most stunning nicoise salads that I have ever eaten have been in the South of France, looking out over the beautiful waters of the Mediterranean Sea. This variation on this famous salad includes grilled pancetta and a lower fat alternative for the dressing.

A Japanese variation of the nicoise can also be made with seared tuna. Coat loin tuna with wasabi paste and black sesame seeds. Sear for approximately 20-30 seconds on each side and allow to cool. Slice into approximately 1 cm slices and add to the salad.

Dressing:
100 mls olive oil
40 mls sherry vinegar
salt and pepper

1.2 kg new season gourmet salad potatoes, cleaned
250 g green beans, topped and tailed
6 paper-thin slices pancetta
200 g baby spinach
½ cup cherry tomatoes, halved
4 hard-boiled eggs, quartered
4 anchovy fillets, halved
handful of chopped chives

Combine the dressing ingredients and set aside.

Cook the potatoes in salted water. Drain, slice and chill them. Blanch the beans in salted boiling water for 5-7 minutes and refresh them in ice water.

Remove any excess fat from the pancetta, then grill until slightly browned but still retaining its shape. Drain on absorbent paper towels. Once cool, slice the pancetta into thirds.

Assemble all the salad ingredients: the spinach with the beans, potatoes, cooked pancetta, tomatoes, eggs, anchovies and chives. Then dress.

Thai Noodle Salad
Serves 6

Any type of noodles will do for this recipe but I like to use the dried egg noodles sold at supermarkets in bags of about 12 bundles: 200 g equates to approximately 2 bundles.

Approximately 200 g noodles, cooked, drained and cooled
2 tablespoons grapeseed oil
1 onion, finely sliced
1 clove garlic, diced
2 stalks lemongrass, finely diced
1 cm piece ginger, shredded
1 red and 1 green capsicum, both halved, seeded and membranes removed and finely sliced

75 mls light soy sauce
50 mls fish sauce
juice of 1 lemon
salt and pepper
2 tablespoons chopped fresh mint
2 tablespoons chopped fresh coriander

In a wok, heat the oil. Add the onion, garlic, lemongrass and ginger and sauté until the onion is tender. Add the capsicums and sauté. Add the soy sauce, fish sauce, lemon juice and salt and pepper. Stir until the sauce has reduced and slightly thickened. (Depending on your wok and the temperature, this should take 5-7 minutes.) Add the chopped fresh herbs, then the drained noodles and toss and heat through.

Tomato Bread Salad
Serves 6

This is an Italian classic. The bread, preferably ciabatta or similar white bread, needs to be 1-2 days old. The crusts should be removed and the bread cubed.

1 large loaf of bread, cubed
1 cup halved cherry tomatoes
approximately 200 g baby spinach
1 small red onion, finely sliced
½ cucumber, peeled, seeded and diced

Dressing:
2 tablespoons capers
6 anchovies, halved
½ cup olive oil
juice of 1 lemon
60 mls red wine vinegar
a few fresh basil leaves
salt and pepper

Combine all the salad ingredients.

Combine all the dressing ingredients. Toss the dressing with the salad ingredients and allow to rest a good 4-5 hours before serving.

Vine-ripened tomatoes
For salads and dishes that call for fresh tomatoes only use ones ripened on the vine. These have flavour that the others just don't.

sweets

This chapter covers a lot of ground, including everything from a humble traditional scone to the glory of the exotic, spiced, roasted pineapple. There's a sweet for every occasion: biscuits to accompany a morning cup of coffee, cakes for office shouts and parties, and desserts for the most swept-up of dinner parties.

baking is an adventure and I like to try new things. Along with the mandatory favourites (and who could go past our Zarbo Chocolate Brownie, of which I have put in a berry variation) there are some different and interesting ideas for desserts combining unusual ingredients – Chargrilled Summer Stone Fruits with Lime, Basil, Rum and Rosemary (p.127), or Cottage Cheesecake with Lemoncello (p.102), for example.

Lots of my Zarbo customers have a sweet tooth. Morning and afternoon tea-time sees consumption of our most popular sweets skyrocket, so of course I had to include some of these recipes. There are also several delicious treats for people on wheat-free diets.

Baking does tend to be more of an exact science than cooking – you do need to follow measurements and baking times carefully so things turn out as they're supposed to. This doesn't mean you can't be creative with presentation, though. The cupcakes are a case in point: the decoration can be as outrageous as you like. Have fun – a little imagination can go a long way.

Handmade Ricotta Cheese

Makes approximately 2 cups

I think by making this fresh you get a much nicer flavour than store-bought alternatives provide. Use it in baking, pasta or any other recipe that calls for ricotta. It is important to strain the curd thoroughly: if it is too wet it will fall apart.

300 mls cream
2 litres full-cream milk
juice of 1 lemon
pinch of salt

Gently bring the cream and milk to the boil with the lemon juice and salt. Reduce heat and simmer for approximately 10-15 minutes. The mixture splits and creates a curd. To strain, place the curd in a piece of clean muslin and tie a knot at the top. Through the knot, thread the handle of a wooden spoon and suspend over a bowl, allowing the liquid to fully drain from the curd. Allow approximately 2-3 hours for this.

Caramelised Pineapple with Ginger and Oriental Spices
Serves 8-10

This stunning dessert is a variation of a dish served at the Villa St Elme in Saint Tropez. The aroma as it is cooking is amazing. I suggest removing the crown of the pineapple and reattaching before serving. Serve with a citrus gelato.

1 pineapple with crown
75 g caster sugar
1 vanilla pod, spilt lengthways, retaining the seeds
2 cinnamon sticks
6 whole star anise
2 cm piece of ginger, finely sliced
150 mls Cointreau
juice of 4 limes

Remove the crown from the pineapple and retain. (After cooking and cooling, reattach the crown using toothpicks.) Peel the pineapple, removing all skin and spikes.

In a large pan, allow the sugar to caramelise over a low heat until light brown, then add the whole peeled pineapple, spices and ginger. Sauté the pineapple until well covered with syrup on all sides. Add the Cointreau, and ignite to burn off the alcohol. Add the lime juice and simmer for approximately 30 minutes, turning the pineapple regularly and basting with the sauce. Allow to cool in the pan.

'Hello Rosie' Slice

When cut, makes 18 slices

This Zarbo variation on a classic Texan slice is rich but not too sweet. I recommend that you use only good quality, fresh walnuts.

100 g butter, melted
250 g malt biscuits, crushed
2 cups walnut pieces, chopped roughly and lightly toasted
1½ cups dark chocolate buttons, chopped
1 cup sultanas
3 cups long thread coconut
500 g sweetened condensed milk

Mix together the butter and biscuit crumbs and press into a 20 x 30 cm slice tin, greased and lined with baking paper.

Mix together the remaining ingredients and roughly press over base. Bake at 160°C for 30 minutes or until browned. Don't overcook. The finished product should be slightly moist and sticky. If the slice starts to brown too quickly during the cooking time, cover with baking paper until the time is up. Cut when cold.

Chocolate Celebration Cake
Serves at least 12

This is a light-textured cake, perfect for cutting and building into all sorts of shapes, for all sorts of celebrations, with the ganache acting as a superb 'glue'. Together it all just tastes divine.

450 g plain flour
1½ cups Dutch cocoa
½ teaspoon salt
1 teaspoon baking powder
3 teaspoons baking soda
3 eggs
2½ cups caster sugar
1 cup oil
2 teaspoons vanilla essence
double shot short espresso or ⅓ cup very strong black coffee
1½ tablespoons white vinegar
2 cups water

Syrup:
½ cup sugar
½ cup water
½ cup whisky or brandy

Chocolate ganache:
250 g cream
350 g dark chocolate buttons

Sift together the flour, cocoa, salt, baking powder and baking soda. Beat together the eggs and sugar, then add the oil, vanilla, espresso, vinegar and water and mix thoroughly. With an electric mixer, beat the dry mixture into the wet mixture until smooth.

Spoon into a greased, lined 26 cm cake tin. Bake at 180° for 1½ hours.

For the syrup, place the sugar, water and whisky or brandy in a saucepan, heating gently until the sugar is melted. Simmer for 1 minute. Pour this mixture over the hot cake as soon as it is pulled from oven.

You can make the ganache in one of two ways:

1) Put the cream and dark chocolate buttons in a microwave bowl and heat for 1 minute, stir, then heat again for 1 minute. Mix until smooth and combined. Refrigerate.

2) Heat the cream in a saucepan to boiling point (but don't boil). Cool slightly, then add the chocolate buttons and leave to sit for 1 minute. Mix until smooth, then refrigerate.

When the cake is cold, ice the top and sides with the chocolate ganache, using a palate knife. Decorate as desired. (You can do this with icing writing, silver balls and candles, etc.)

Chocolate Macaroons
Makes 12 macaroons

These biscuits are gluten- and wheat-free, but not dairy-free. Use only a good quality dark chocolate. I recommend chocolate with 71% cocoa mass as it provides a superior flavour. These really are very good.

250 g good dark chocolate
2 egg whites
pinch of salt
¾ cup caster sugar
1 teaspoon vanilla essence
2 cups long thread coconut

Roughly chop the chocolate and place in a heatproof bowl. Melt over a saucepan of simmering water, but don't allow the bottom of the bowl to touch the water. Watch and stir constantly, so chocolate does not overheat and burn. Then allow the melted chocolate to cool slightly (the consistency should be smooth and still runny).

Put egg whites, salt and ½ cup of sugar into a clean grease-free bowl and whisk until stiff. Then add the rest of the sugar in 3 lots, whisking for a few minutes in between each. Mix in vanilla and the cooled chocolate. Lastly, carefully fold in the coconut.

Spoon tablespoonfuls onto a tray lined with baking paper. Bake at 150°C for 15 minutes until crisp on the outside but still soft and chewy in the centre . . . mmmm.

Variation:
Substitute a good quality white chocolate for the dark chocolate and add ½ cup diced dried apricots.

As our palates have developed, so has our taste for darker chocolate. Cocoa was first cultivated by the ancient Mayans, for whom it was sacred. Today the best chocolate comes from France and Belgium and is readily available in specialty food stores here.

Cottage Cheesecake with Lemoncello
Serves 10-12

This is a low-fat, less rich alternative to a traditional cheesecake. You can use either cottage cheese or the Handmade Ricotta (p.93). Lemoncello is a stunning lemon liqueur traditionally made in Italy. If it's unavailable you can substitute lemon juice and zest. Keep the lemoncello in the freezer and try it on ice, over gelato or in a glass of champagne.

Italian pastry:
70 g butter, cut into cubes
350 g plain flour
100 g sugar
pinch of salt
100 g olive oil
70 mls water

Filling:
1.5 kg cottage cheese or handmade ricotta (p.93) (or a combination)
6 eggs
125 g butter, melted
1½ cups sugar
½ cup lemoncello (or lemon zest and juice)
1 cup flour
1 cup mixed peel
½ cup dried apricots
1 cup sultanas

For the pastry, rub the butter into the flour, sugar and salt. This should resemble fine breadcrumbs. Then add the oil and water, mixing to make a smooth dough.

Grease a 26 cm spring-form cake pan and line base and sides with the pastry. The pastry is easier to handle by pressing into pan. Refrigerate while preparing the filling.

For the filling, place cottage cheese in a mixing bowl and beat for 1 minute to smooth a little. Add the ingredients in the order listed, combining well after each addition, but fold through the dried fruit carefully. Pour into the prepared pastry case. Bake at 180°C for 1 hour to 1 hour 20 minutes, until set.

Pistachio and Ginger Slice
When cut, makes 18 squares

Another classic slice and a Zarbo favourite. This recipe will make quite a high slice which can be cut into thick wedges. Lightly toasting the nuts before using brings out their flavour and creates a superior finish.

1 cup slivered almonds
½ cup hazelnuts, chopped
3 cups plain flour
1 teaspoon baking powder
3 teaspoons ground ginger
300 g butter
1½ cups brown sugar

Icing:
125 g butter
200 g golden syrup
3 teaspoons ground ginger
1 cup mixed peel
3 cups icing sugar

Garnish:
100 g lightly toasted pistachio nuts, roughly chopped

Toast the slivered almonds and chopped hazelnuts in the oven at 180°C for approximately 10 minutes. Keep an eye on them to make sure they don't burn.

Sift together the flour, baking powder, ginger.

In a separate bowl, beat together the butter and sugar. Mix in the sifted dry ingredients and then the cooled almonds and hazelnuts. Press into a greased and lined 30 x 20 cm slice tin. Bake at 180°C for 15 minutes until cooked through.

For the icing melt the butter and golden syrup over a saucepan of simmering water, then stir in the ginger, peel and icing sugar and mix until smooth. While the base is still hot, spread the topping over evenly and scatter with the toasted pistachio nuts.

Cut when cold.

Lemon Meringue Tarts
Makes 10 individual tarts

Once you've made the pastry and lemon curd these are easy tarts to whisk up in a short time. The meringue always looks so impressive. Serve with afternoon tea or as a dessert. If you're making the butterscotch variation, dark muscovado sugar really does provide a gorgeous flavour.

400 g sweet short pastry (below)
6 egg whites
150 g sugar
1 teaspoon vanilla essence
approximately 400 g lemon curd (below)

Knead and roll pastry on a floured surface to ½ cm thickness. Line 10 individual greased tart rings (or use a Texan muffin tin to make deeper tarts) with the pastry and prick the bottoms with a fork.

Cover with tin foil, pushing the foil down into the edges. Refrigerate for 15-20 minutes. Bake at 180°C for 8 minutes. Remove foil and bake for a further 3 minutes. Pastry should be cooked but not browned. Cool.

In a bowl, mix the egg whites and 50 g of the sugar and whisk until stiff peaks form, then add the remaining sugar in 2 lots, whisking well in between until the meringue is smooth and glossy. Fold in the vanilla essence.

Spoon the lemon curd into the cooked pastry bases. Then pile the meringue mixture high over the curd. Bake at 150°C for 10 minutes or until brown.

Variation:
Butterscotch Meringue Tarts

400 g chocolate pastry (see sweet short pastry, below)
150 g organic Indian sukkah (or dark muscovado sugar)
2 egg yolks
1 teaspoon vanilla essence
60 g butter
40 g cornflour
200 g cream

Line individual tart rings with chocolate pastry and bake as for lemon meringue tarts.

Put all remaining ingredients in a heatproof bowl and place over a saucepan of simmering water to melt, stirring constantly as for lemon meringue tarts. Stir until the mixture thickens and is smooth (about 10-15 minutes).

Spoon into the cooked pastry cases and pile on the meringue as for the lemon meringue tarts. Bake at 150°C for 10 minutes or until brown.

Lemon Curd
Makes approximately 600 g
This curd is for the lemon meringue tarts but is great as a preserve with toasted bagels.

300 g sugar
200 g butter, diced
3 organic lemons, zest and juice
3 eggs, whisked

Place the sugar and diced butter in a heatproof bowl and place over a saucepan of simmering water. Do not let the bowl touch the water. Stir until the butter is melted and the sugar is dissolved. Remove the bowl from heat and allow to cool a bit, then mix in the lemon juice and zest.

When mixture is just warm (if it's too hot, it will cook the eggs), stir in the whisked eggs. Place back over the saucepan of simmering water and stir constantly until curd starts to thicken, but not curdle. (This takes approximately 10-15 minutes.)

Store in the refrigerator for up to 2 weeks.

Sweet Short Pastry
Makes enough for 10 individual tarts or one 28 cm tart

For meringue tarts and the chocolate tart recipes

200 g butter, softened
150 g icing sugar
2 eggs
400 g plain flour, sifted

Cream butter and icing sugar together. Beat in eggs one at a time. Mix in the flour. Remove from the processor or bowl and knead until well-combined. Pat the dough into a ball, then wrap in cling film and refrigerate for 30 minutes before using.

Variation:
For chocolate sweet pastry replace 75 g of flour with Dutch cocoa.

Orange Almond Cake
Serves 12

We've been making this cake at Zarbo since day one. Although it's not originally a Zarbo recipe, I've included it because it is wonderfully flavoursome. Boiling the oranges really intensifies their flavour. As this cake contains no flour or dairy products it's ideal for people who need to exclude wheat, gluten and dairy products from their diet. To make it stand out, try it as a dessert with the Burnt Orange Sauce (p.111) and some mascarpone.

3 whole oranges
250 g caster sugar
9 eggs
2 teaspoons baking powder or gluten-, wheat- and dairy-free raising agent (p.113 or available from health food shops)
650 g ground almonds
3 tablespoons apricot jam
a little hot water

Cover the oranges with water and bring to the boil. Turn down the heat and simmer for approximately 20 minutes. Discard the water and purée the whole oranges in a blender to pulp.

Whisk together the sugar and eggs until thick. Carefully fold in the baking powder (or raising agent), the ground almonds and puréed orange pulp.

Pour the mixture into a loose-bottomed 26 cm cake tin which has been greased and lined with baking paper. Bake at 180°C for 1 hour. This cake does need the full hour; if it starts to brown on top during the cooking time cover with baking paper.

For the glaze, heat the jam and hot water to make a thick, spreadable syrup. Brush the glaze over the top of the warm cake.

Serve with Burnt Orange Sauce (p.111) and mascarpone.

Roasted Rhubarb with Kaffir Lime and Ginger Syrup

Makes approximately ⅔ of a cup

This is a stunningly simple and quickly prepared dessert. Roasting the rhubarb takes a couple of minutes but as it caramelises its flavour intensifies. I recommend serving this with mascarpone and perhaps some crushed amaretti biscuits.

The syrup can be made in advance. Versatile and long lasting in the fridge, it can also be used on pancakes, on french toast and even on meat such as pork or lamb.

Syrup:
1 cm piece ginger (approximately 15-20 g), peeled and shredded
4 large kaffir lime leaves, finely shredded
½ cup cold water
½ cup sugar
juice of 2 large limes

6 stalks of rhubarb, cleaned and cut into approximately 10 cm pieces
½ cup caster sugar

Place all the ingredients for the syrup in a heavy-based saucepan and bring to the boil. Reduce the heat and simmer until the mixture thickens (approximately 4-6 minutes). This can be made in advance.

Place rhubarb on a baking tray, sprinkle with the sugar, then bake in a moderate oven (about 160°C) for approximately 8-10 minutes.

Place the rhubarb on a plate and drizzle with the syrup.

Rosemary and Balsamic Syrup
Makes 1 cup

This syrup is fantastic with a range of different cakes such as the Lemon Almond Cake (p.126) or a polenta cake. Try it over pancakes or even over roasted vegetables.

1½ cups water
2 cups caster sugar
½ cup balsamic vinegar
50 g fresh rosemary needles, removed from stem

In a saucepan bring the water to boiling point. Add the sugar and vinegar. Allow the sugar to dissolve, stirring slightly. Add the rosemary and simmer uncovered for approximately 15 minutes until liquid is a syrupy consistency and rosemary is infused. Strain.

Burnt Orange Sauce
Makes approximately 1½ cups

This sauce should accompany the Orange Almond Cake (p.108), but is also ideal for pancakes, french toast, etc.

1 cup muscovado sugar
½ cup caster sugar
juice and rind of 3 oranges
½ cup Cointreau

Put all the ingredients in a heavy-based saucepan and bring to the boil. Reduce heat and simmer uncovered for approximately 30 minutes. Strain, reserving the liquid.

Pomegranate Syrup

Fresh pomegranates are pretty hard to find in New Zealand, but if you do find them you might like to try this beautifully coloured syrup. It goes wonderfully on pancakes, ice cream or your favourite dessert.

2 whole pomegranates
½ cup cold water
½ cup sugar

Cut the pomegranates in half. Remove and retain the seeds and juice. Place these in a heavy-based saucepan with the water and sugar and bring to the boil. Reduce the heat and simmer until the mixture is thickened (approximately 4-6 minutes). Strain the syrup to remove the pulp but still retain the seeds.

A Variation of the Famous Zarbo Chocolate Brownie

When cut, makes approximately 20 pieces

A deli book couldn't possibly exist without a brownie recipe and this variation of the classic Zarbo version is just so good. We've added raspberries and almonds to make it extra special.

300 g dark chocolate, chopped
300 g butter, diced
1½ cups plain flour
½ cup Dutch cocoa
2 cups sugar
6 eggs
2 teaspoons vanilla essence
½ cup slivered almonds, toasted
1 cup fresh or frozen raspberries

In a heatproof bowl melt the chocolate and butter over a saucepan of simmering water (do not let the bowl touch the water), mix until smooth and allow to cool until just warm.

Sift together the flour and cocoa.

In a separate bowl whisk together the sugar and eggs until thick and creamy, but not too thick. Mix in vanilla essence and chocolate mixture until smooth. Fold in the sifted flour and cocoa, then pour into a greased 20 x 30 cm slice tin. Sprinkle the raspberries and nuts evenly on top.

Bake at 170°C for 25 minutes or until a skewer comes out clean at the edges but gooey in centre. It is important not to overcook the brownie. You may have to experiment a bit with the cooking time to get the brownie just as you like it.

When cool, cut into squares.

Gluten-, Wheat- and Dairy-Free Muffins

Makes 12 muffins

After much experimentation, we developed this recipe for people with dairy, gluten and wheat allergies. Use it as a base and come up with your own flavours. Use lots of fruit and fruit pulp.

You can either buy a gluten-, wheat- and dairy-free raising agent available from health shops or make your own. I've reproduced a good recipe here from *The Allergy Bible*, published by Quadrille Publishing Ltd.

Wheat-free Baking Powder:
60 g sodium bicarbonate
130 g cream of tartar
60 g non-wheat flour
Mix all the ingredients and sieve together thoroughly.

3 cups medium ground polenta
1 teaspoon cinnamon
1 cup ground almonds
2 teaspoons gluten-, wheat-, dairy-free raising agent
4 ripe bananas, mashed
1½ cups raw organic sugar
4 eggs
1 tablespoon lemon juice
1 teaspoon vanilla essence
zest of 1 orange
½ cup grapeseed oil
1 cup of fruit pulp, perhaps

apricot
2 cups of fruit (fresh or frozen berries work best)

Sift together the polenta, cinnamon, ground almonds and raising agent. In a large bowl mash the bananas and mix in the sugar. Then add the eggs, lemon juice, vanilla, orange zest, oil and fruit pulp and mix till combined. Add the dry ingredients to this mixture and then lastly fold through the 2 cups of fruit. Spoon the mixture into a muffin tray lined with paper cases and bake at 180°C for 25-30 minutes, or until set, but not overcooked. As with all muffins, cooking times will vary with individual ovens.

Sicilian Apple Cake
Serves 10-12

This cake may appear a bit complex at the outset but it is well worth the effort. It has a moist custardy texture and makes a great dessert, served with a large dollop of mascarpone.

50 g walnut pieces
120 g butter, melted
½ kg apples, sliced and cored
½ a lemon, zest and juice
150 g plain flour
1½ teaspoons baking powder
3 eggs
250 g sugar
1 teaspoon vanilla essence
100 mls milk
¼ cup raisins
⅛ cup pine nuts
1 tablespoon brown sugar
1 teaspoon cinnamon

Toast the walnuts in the oven at 170°C for approximately 10 minutes. Keep an eye on them to make sure they don't burn. Line a 23 cm cake tin with baking paper. Pour a little of the melted butter into the tin and sprinkle over toasted walnuts.

In a bowl, mix the sliced apples with the lemon zest and juice.

In a separate bowl, sift together the flour and baking powder.

In a third bowl, whisk together the eggs, sugar and vanilla essence. Mix in the milk and the rest of the butter. Then add the sifted dry ingredients and mix until smooth.

Pour half the batter over the walnuts in the prepared cake tin. Arrange half of the apples and juice over the batter, then sprinkle over half of the raisins. Repeat with the rest of the batter, then apples, then raisins. Lastly, sprinkle on the pine nuts, brown sugar and cinnamon.

Bake at 170° for 1-1½ hours. This cake may take a little longer than that to cook: it should be set but still moist. Use your judgement. Cover the top with baking paper if it begins to brown during baking.

Cupcakes
Makes 12

Cupcakes are another classic that have made a return. I was first inspired to try them out at Zarbo after seeing them some years ago in a New York café called Cupcake. These are a much lighter version than the old-fashioned ones. The passionfruit pulp supplies a nice fruity zing, which should be outdone only by your choice of icing. These cakes are ideal for a kids' birthday party. If you're entertaining, try making mini-cupcakes.

6 eggs
150 g brown sugar
100 g caster sugar
350 g butter, melted
2 tablespoons milk
2 tablespoons lemon juice
2 tablespoons passionfruit pulp
350 g self-raising flour

Icing:
200 g butter
400 g icing sugar
1 tablespoon lemon juice
boiling water
a few drops of food dye

Whisk the eggs and sugars together. Mix in the butter, then the milk, lemon juice and passionfruit pulp. Finally, stir in the self-raising flour and mix until smooth.

Spoon the mixture into muffin tins lined with paper cases. Bake at 180° for 25-30 minutes.

For the icing, cream the butter and sugar until light and fluffy. Mix in the lemon juice and enough water to beat to a light and spreadable consistency. Colour with food dye and decorate with jellybeans or sugar flowers or coloured sugar or silver balls. Be creative!

Iced Hazelnut Shortbread
Makes 18

This is a versatile recipe: you can
make a batch just to have as
shortbread or you can make it a bit
more glam for party food.

Shortbread:
250 g butter, softened
½ cup caster sugar
180 g ground hazelnuts
2 teaspoons lemon juice
2⅔ cups plain flour

Fondant icing:
2 egg whites
2 cups icing sugar
1 teaspoon glucose syrup

a little hot water
a few drops of food colouring

Cream the butter and sugar until smooth and light. Mix in the
hazelnuts and lemon juice. Then add the flour and mix to make a
smooth dough.

On a floured surface, knead the dough into a ball, then roll out to
1 cm thickness. Cut with a variety of shaped cutters and place on a
baking tray lined with baking paper.

Bake at 180°C for 10-15 minutes until golden brown. Cool before
icing.

For the icing, mix together the egg whites and icing sugar, add the
glucose syrup and mix until smooth. (If the mixture is too thick, add a
little water. If too thin, add a little more icing sugar.) Colour with food
colouring. Pipe the fondant icing onto cold biscuits and decorate for
any occasion.

Date and Orange Scones
Makes 12

This recipe is fantastic for morning tea or brunch. You can use any dried fruit here, but dates are definitely the classic favourite. If you like lots of fruit in scones, increase the quantity of dates to 2 cups and the peel to about 1 cup.

1½ cups dried dates, chopped
½ cup mixed peel
½ cup orange juice
4 cups plain flour
1 tablespoon caster sugar
4 teaspoons baking powder
2 teaspoons ground cinnamon
100 g cold butter, cut into cubes
approximately ½ cup milk

Combine the dates, mixed peel and orange juice and leave to soak for 2 hours or overnight.

Sift together the flour, sugar, baking powder and cinnamon. Rub in the butter. Stir in the date/peel mixture and milk; for easier and faster mixing, use a metal spoon. Mix until just combined (the metal spoon will help you not to overmix) and form a dough.

Pat carefully into a flat rectangle on a floured surface and cut into 12 triangle shapes. Sprinkle with coffee sugar crystals and bake on a flat lined tray at 200°C for 20 minutes.

Eat hot with loads of butter!

Zarbo Deli and Cafe is a one-stop shop for real foodies. Tradition and innovation are equally important to us and we invest a lot of time travelling the world to find products and ideas to bring back to New Zealand.

Eccles Cakes
Makes 12

Eccles Cakes are a British classic. This particular recipe is a very traditional one, perfected by Zarbo's head baker, Sallyann Hingston, whilst working in the UK. Great served warm with a wedge of good crumbly English cheddar – delicious.

325 g brown sugar
200 g butter
500 g currants
3 teaspoons ground allspice
3 teaspoons ground nutmeg
500 g puff pastry
1 egg
caster sugar

In a heatproof bowl over a saucepan of simmering water, melt together the butter and brown sugar. Remove from the heat and mix in the spices and currants. Set aside.

Roll out the pastry on a floured surface to a 1 cm thickness. Using a 8 cm round cutter, cut out circles of the pastry and discard any scraps (as these are now unusable). Take a tablespoon full of the currant mixture, gently press into a ball in your hands and then place on top of the pastry round. Encase the fruit with the outer edges of the pastry, pushing the pastry edges together to completely enclose the fruit. Turn over and roll slightly to form into an even flat round disc. Score the top with a sharp knife 3 times and place on a baking tray lined with baking paper. Repeat the process with the rest of the pastry and currant mixture.

Lightly whisk 1 egg with a little water and then brush on top of the Eccles Cakes. Sprinkle each cake with a teaspoon of caster sugar, then bake at 190°C for approximately 15-20 minutes.

They should puff up, be golden brown and oozing slightly.

Puff Pastry

For ease buy commercially produced puff pastry from the supermarket. If, however, you'd like to attempt your own, the recipe follows.

500 g flour (strong flour for bread baking is best)
½ teaspoon salt
125 g butter, diced and at room temperature
250 mls water
375 g butter, softened

In a large bowl mix together the flour and salt. Rub the 125 g diced butter into the flour until the mixture resembles fine breadcrumbs. Tip the mixture out onto a large work surface (a stainless steel bench or piece of marble is best) and make a well in the centre. Carefully pour all of the water into the well and start mixing the flour and water together to form a ball of dough. Try not to overwork: mix and knead together until just combined. Cover with cling film and allow to rest for 20 minutes.

Cut the 375 g of butter into 1 cm slabs, making sure it is evenly softened. On a floured surface roll the pastry out to a square shape about 2 cm thick. Spread slabs of the softened butter over the centre of the pastry, leaving a border of about 5 cm all around.

Then fold over the border to encase all of the butter, so none is exposed. Roll the pastry one way into a long rectangle, then fold the ends over to make 3 layers. Turn 90 degrees and roll again, folding the ends over into 3 layers.

Cover and rest for 20 minutes. Repeat the double rolling process another 2 times, resting in between each turn. Now the puff pastry is ready to use.

Panforte

When cut, makes 30 fingers

Panforte dates back about a thousand years to the monks of Siena. It has become another deli classic which is served in thin slices with coffee. Don't be shocked by the addition of the pepper: it gives the spice to the slice.

250 g whole blanched almonds
250 g whole hazelnuts, skins on
175 g flour
60 g cocoa
2 teaspoons cinnamon
⅔ teaspoon white ground pepper
125 g dried diced apricots

125 g glacé cherries
125 g mixed peel
120 g dark chocolate, chopped
⅔ cup caster sugar
1 cup runny honey

Place the almonds and hazelnuts in a shallow pan with sides and toast in a slow oven (approximately 140°C), until slightly brown (about 20 minutes), shaking several times to prevent burning on any point.

In a large bowl sift and mix well the flour, cocoa, cinnamon and pepper. Mix in the nuts and fruit.

In a heatproof bowl over a saucepan of simmering water, melt together the chocolate, sugar and honey, stirring until smooth. (Do not let the bowl touch the water.)

Stir the chocolate mixture into the dry mixture until thoroughly combined. Press into a 30 x 20 cm greased slice tin lined with baking paper. Bake at 180°C for 25 minutes. Be careful not to overcook the mixture; the baked panforte will still look quite soft and, when cool, should have a slightly chewy texture.

Espresso Cream

Serves 4

This is a café twist on the old Kiwi favourite Spanish Cream, which was made with almond essence and pink food colouring, then put into Agee jars and taken on picnics! This variation has a strong coffee zing but a lovely light, delicate texture similar to panacotta. Complemented by curls of good chocolate, it is perfect for light summer eating.

3 cups full-cream milk
1½ tablespoons gelatine powder or
3 gelatine sheets
1 shot of espresso, or ½ cup of
very strong black coffee
1 vanilla pod, cut in half and
shed seeds, set seeds aside
3 eggs, separated
½ cup caster sugar
curls of good chocolate for garnish
(grate chocolate with a potato
peeler)

Dissolve the gelatine powder in 1 cup of the milk or, if using gelatine sheets, soak in water until supple.

In a saucepan place the remaining 2 cups of milk, the espresso and vanilla pod and seeds, heat until hot but not boiling. Remove from the heat and discard the vanilla pod. Allow to cool for a few minutes.

Whisk together the egg yolks and sugar. Then slowly whisk in the hot milk mixture. Whisk to an even consistency. Add the soaked gelatine and milk mixture. Mix until all is combined.

In a separate bowl, whisk the egg whites until soft peaks form, then fold carefully into the milk mixture.

Pour into individual glasses or a large glass serving bowl. Refrigerate for at least 2 hours to set. Garnish with chocolate curls.

Almond Nougat and Lemon Biscotti

Makes approximately 30

Biscotti is Italian for biscuits. They have been traced back to ancient Roman times when they were eaten on festive occasions. Try these modern Zarbo variations with a really good cup of coffee.

4 eggs
250 g caster sugar
⅓ cup lemoncello, or zest of 2 lemons
pinch of salt
500 g self-raising flour, sifted
200 g almond nougat, coarsely chopped (choose a hard variety)
1 teaspoon nutmeg
1 beaten egg

Whisk together the eggs and sugar until thick, add the lemoncello or zest, and salt. Fold in the sifted flour, chopped nougat and nutmeg until just combined to form a dough.

Divide the mixture in half. On a floured surface roll each piece into a log approximately 5 cm wide. Place on a lined baking tray and brush with a beaten egg. Bake at 180°C for 35 minutes.

When cold, cut the logs on an angle into pieces ½ cm thick. Lay out flat on a baking tray and bake again in low oven until crisp (approximately 15 minutes).

Variations:
Orange and Rosemary
zest and juice of 3 oranges
½ cup finely chopped rosemary

Add both these ingredients to the whisked eggs and sugar and follow the method above.

Pistachio and Cardamom
zest of 1 lemon
200 g pistachio nuts
2 teaspoons ground cardamom

Add the lemon zest to the eggs and sugar, and the pistachio nuts and ground cardamom to the flour. Then follow the method above.

Lemon Almond Cake
Serves 10-12

Ideal for afternoon tea, this cake has a light madeira texture. The combination of almond and lemon gives a delicate and subtle flavour. To turn this into a dessert, serve it warmed slightly with a drizzle of Rosemary and Balsamic Syrup (p.111) and mascarpone.

2 cups plain flour
2 teaspoons baking powder
pinch of salt
150 g almond paste at room temperature
125 g butter at room temperature
½ cup caster sugar
4 eggs
1 teaspoon vanilla essence
3 lemons, zest and juice
½ cup milk

Lemon icing:
2 teaspoons butter
1½ cups icing sugar
1 dessertspoon lemon juice
a little hot water

Mix together the flour, baking powder and salt.

In a separate bowl, beat together the almond paste, butter and sugar until smooth. Add the eggs one at a time, then the vanilla, lemon zest and juice.

Add the mixed dry ingredients to the butter mixture in 3 lots, alternating with the milk, mix until smooth. Spoon into a greased and floured ring tin.

Bake at 180°C for 30-40 minutes. When cool, drizzle with the lemon icing.

For the icing, mix together the butter and icing sugar. Then add in the lemon juice and enough hot water to mix to a smooth runny consistency for pouring over the cooled cake.

Chargrilled Summer Stone Fruits with Lime, Basil, Rum and Rosemary

Serves 6

This is the perfect ending for a summer party. The combination of the sweetness of the fruit with the citrus of the lime and the spice of the rum, rosemary and basil will blow your guests away. The fruit can also be served with the Kaffir Lime and Ginger Syrup (p.110).

For this recipe the fruit should be ripe but not overripe. Once cooked it should retain its shape. Experiment with different fruit, perhaps introducing something tropical such as papaya. Whatever you decide on, though, choose fruit that's full of colour.

4 peaches, quartered
4 nectarines, quartered
4 apricots, quartered
4 juicy plums, quartered
2 limes, cut into wedges
1 teaspoon chopped fresh rosemary
50 mls rum
1 tablespoon chopped basil

Combine the fruits with the rosemary and the rum.

Grill on a hot, clean grill for only a few minutes, turning over once. It is important that the fruit retains its shape and texture. The limes will need to be grilled for slightly longer than the other fruits, simply because they are harder and this will bring more juice out of them.

Top with chopped basil.

French Chocolate Tart
Serves 12

This tart is decadent, rich and velvety in texture. Once again I recommend that you use only good quality 71% dark chocolate. If you use inferior chocolate, the tart will not set. You can turn this into quite an impressive creation by garnishing with chocolate shards.

Please note the short cooking time. It does come out of the oven looking uncooked, but it will set once refrigerated.

Chocolate pastry (see Sweet Short Pastry p.105)

Filling:
300 g 71% dark chocolate, chopped
200 g butter
3 eggs
5 egg yolks
75 g caster sugar
1 tablespoon Kahlua liqueur or coffee essence

Line a 28 cm tart tin with the chocolate pastry, then cover with tin foil, pushing the foil carefully into edges of the tin. Refrigerate for 20 minutes then bake at 190°C for 10 minutes. Remove the foil and bake a further 5 minutes. The shell should be cooked through, not crumbly or dry.

Place the chocolate and butter in a heatproof bowl and set over a saucepan of simmering water. Note that the water should not touch the bottom of the bowl – the chocolate and butter are melted by the rising steam only. Allow to cool to a warm temperature. (If the chocolate is too hot it will cause the whisked eggs to collapse when they're combined.)

In a separate bowl, whisk the whole eggs, egg yolks and sugar until just thick and creamy. Fold in the cooled chocolate mix and Kahlua, then pour into the pre-baked chocolate tart shell.

Bake at 140°C for 15 minutes only. The tart will still be very runny after baking, but once cold it will set and have a lovely mousse-like texture. Refrigerate to help set but this tart is best eaten at room temperature. Cut into at least 12 wedges, as it is extremely rich. Decorate with shards of chocolate and a dusting of cocoa if desired.

Chocolate shards:
200 g white chocolate buttons
200 g dark chocolate shards

In separate bowls over saucepans of boiling water, melt the white and dark chocolate buttons (which in this instance work better than other chocolate).

Line a large flat tray with baking paper. Spread the tray with the slightly cooled white chocolate, then drizzle over the melted dark chocolate. Fold the paper and chocolate onto itself and then peel apart to make a swirled, textured look. Set in the refrigerator, then break up and use to decorate the top of the tart.

index